CCNA Exam Preparation

Editor in Chief: Stephen Helba
Assistant Vice President and Publisher: Charles E. Stewart, Jr.
Production Editor: Alexandrina Benedicto Wolf
Design Coordinator: Diane Ernsberger
Production Manager: Matthew Ottenweller
Cover Designer: Michael R. Hall
Cover Art: Michael R. Hall
Illustrations: Michael R. Hall and Cathy J. Boulay

This book was set in Futura MD BT, Times New Roman, and Arial by Cathy J. Boulay, Marcraft International, Inc. It was printed and bound by R.R. Donnelley & Sons Company. The cover was printed by Phoenix Color Corp.

Pearson Education Ltd., *London*
Pearson Education Australia Pty. Limited, *Sydney*
Pearson Education Singapore, Pte. Ltd.
Pearson Education North Asia Ltd., *Hong Kong*
Pearson Education Canada, Ltd., *Toronto*
Pearson Educacion de Mexico, S.A. de C.V.
Pearson Education–Japan, *Tokyo*
Pearson Education Malaysia, Pte. Ltd.
Pearson Education, *Upper Saddle River, New Jersey*

Marcraft International President: Charles J. Brooks

Written by Jerald A. Dively

10 9 8 7 6 5 4 3 2 1

ISBN 0-13-094386-X

Preface

As a Cisco instructor, I saw a need to condense the CCNA material into a neat little handbook to make your life easier as you prepare for the CCNA examination (640-507). I decided to present only the material that is necessary, and eliminate all the filler that other authors put into their books.

When using this test preparation tool, you must remember that I have provided only the information necessary to pass the examination. What does this mean? Well, it means that you will pass the test, but may not have a detailed understanding of the subject. First things first—pass the test, then go out and get that 30-pound technical book to help you prepare for the real world.

Getting the CCNA certification will open many doors to you that were previously closed. Don't worry if you feel like a "paper CCNA." You will get the job that you want and then, through on-the-job training, you will get the experience needed to keep the job. After all, how does anybody get experience with routers if they are not given the opportunity to try?

There is another group of people out there: those who are already working with routers, but cannot pass the test or are afraid to take it. This book will provide those people with the knowledge to successfully take the test.

ACKNOWLEDGMENTS

I give my acknowledgments to my loving wife Denise and my two wonderful children Nicole and Ashley. Ashley will be taking her CCNA in December and she is only in the 10th grade. I also acknowledge B and R Associates for providing me with the opportunity to write this book and for their assistance and encouragement in the book's preparation. I especially would like to thank Ray and Ben of B and R Associates for their support.

HOW TO USE THIS BOOK

You might ask yourself, "How do I use this Pass IT book?" Well, the explanation is simple. I have designed this book for anyone to study and take the CCNA test, and I will give you pointers throughout.

First, review the chapter objectives, and then read the chapter. Go back to the chapter objectives to see if you can remember the material covered, then read the chapter again. The more times you expose yourself to information, the better chance that the information will remain in your long-term memory.

Each chapter begins with an introduction. This introduction basically takes the objectives and defines them in easy to understand terms. As I start to discuss material you may see some of the information highlighted ***in bold italic letters*** with an "*" preceding the information. Pay very close attention to this information. The likelihood of seeing this information on the test is very high. Not only do I highlight the really important information, but I also place this information in what I call the Exam Tip. Exam Tips are just that, tips to pass the exam. Sometimes I also include a Note to help you further understand the information.

Finally, I have created questions at the end of each chapter to jog your memory. These are important questions because they concentrate on the subject areas that are tested on the CCNA Examination. The questions are only samples that closely resemble actual test content. This book is accompanied by an additional comprehensive CCNA test bank that is sealed on the back cover of the book. The CD testing material was developed to simulate the CCNA Certification Exam testing process and materials to allow students to complete practice tests, determine their weak points, and study more strategically. I will tell you this: You will not be disappointed when it comes time to take the test.

Now, take the test and good luck!

After you take the test, I would appreciate an e-mail at *marketing@mic-inc.com*. Your input will be used to make this book better.

Table of Contents

Chapter 1 The Network

Chapter 2 Switches and Bridges

Chapter 3   Virtual LANs

Chapter 4 Router Configuration and the IOS

Chapter 5 Managing a Cisco Router

Chapter 6 TCP and the Internet Protocol

Chapter 7 IP Routing

Chapter 8   Configuring IPX

Chapter 9   Access Lists

Chapter 10   Wide Area Networking

Index

Chapter 1

The Network

These are the areas that are generally testable on the CCNA examination:

1. Understanding the OSI (Open System Interconnection) model.

2. Identify and describe the functions of each of the seven layers of the OSI model.

3. Understand the benefits of a layered model.

4. Describe the main benefit of the OSI model.

5. Describe connection-oriented and connectionless network services and identify the key differences between them.

Introduction

In this chapter you will learn topics to help you pass the CCNA Exam, such as the setting up and cabling of Cisco devices. Before you set up your network, however, you have to consider some important aspects. First, decide if you will be using 10 Mbps or 100 Mbps on your network. Plan for the future and use the quickest method to transfer data, so that you won't have to change the hardware too often. If you are setting up a new network today, you are probably going to use Category 5 UTP with RJ-45 connections.

You will then read about the OSI model. There are benefits to using a model. Learn these well, specifically what protocols and services are at each layer.

Connection-oriented and connectionless communications occur for a reason. Remember what constitutes each type of communication. Also covered are the attributes of TCP (connection-oriented) and the three methods of flow control.

The five steps of data encapsulation, and where in the OSI model each step occurs, are important areas to memorize and understand.

You will then be given an overview of some basic networking topologies and how Ethernet networks operate.

SETTING UP AND CABLING CISCO DEVICES

Cabling the Ethernet LAN

The IEEE 802.3 standard was designed for a 10 Mbps network that used coax, twisted-pair, and fiber media. In fact the most commonly used 802.X standards for PC based networking are 802.3, 802.5 and 802.2. Now there are two new standards: 802.3u (Fast Ethernet) and 802.3q (Gigabit Ethernet). These standards use twisted-pair and fiber media. You should do the following to create a cost-effective network:

- Try to use 10 Mbps switches at the Access layer to provide good performance at a reasonable price. 100 Mbps links should be used for servers. After all, you don't want to slow down one of the most important pieces of equipment on your network. (You will learn more about the Cisco Three-Layer Model later in this chapter.)

- Using Fast Ethernet between Access layer and Distribution layer switches is another good idea, as 10 Mbps links would create a bottleneck. (You will learn more about Fast Ethernet later in this book.)

- Fast Ethernet should be used between Distribution layer switches and the core. Dual links between distribution and core switches are recommended for redundancy and load balancing.

RJ-45 UTP Connections

There are two different types of UTP to use when designing a network:

- **Straight-Through:** This is when the wires on both cable ends are in the same order. You can use this cable when you connect a router, server, or workstation to a hub or switch. Notice that you use this type when the devices are not the same.

- **Crossover:** On this type, the wires on both cable ends are crossed. You can use the crossover cable when connecting uplinks between switches, connecting hubs to switches, connecting a hub to another hub, connecting a router interface to another router interface, or connecting two PCs together without a hub or switch.

EXAM TIP: Exam questions in this area are usually limited to when you would use the straight-through or the crossover connection. Don't waste your brain cells memorizing more than you need to.

NOTE: If you just don't get it, look at the port and see if it is marked with an "X". Use a straight-through cable when only one of the two ports is designated with an "X". Use a crossover when both ports are designated with an "X" or when neither port has an "X".

Cabling the Wide Area Network

Serial Transmission: WAN serial connectors use serial transmission. This means there is a transmission of one bit at a time over a single channel. Cisco routers use a proprietary 60-pin serial connector, which you must buy from Cisco. Usually Cisco supports dedicated leased lines *using High-Level Data Link Control (HDLC), Point-to-Point Protocol (PPP)*, Integrated Services Digital Network (ISDN), and Frame Relay.

OSI LAYERING BENEFITS AND CONCEPTS

The OSI model, depicted in Figure 1-1, is used to help deal with the networking concepts in separate pieces, making the process simpler. The OSI layering benefits and concepts include the following:

- ***Its primary purpose is to allow different vendors to interoperate.***

- ***It allows changes to occur in one layer without having to change any other layer***.

- It defines the standard interface for the "plug-and-play" multivendor integration.

- It is easier for humans to discuss and learn.

- It standardizes interfaces between layers.

- It reduces complexity, allowing easy programming.

- The layer below another layer provides services to the higher layer.

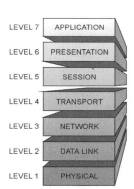

Figure 1-1: OSI Model

Highlights of OSI

Don't get too involved with this section. Memorize the protocols at each layer and what happens at each layer. The upper layers are implemented in software, and the lower layers are based on hardware. This might be a good point to help you remember what action takes place at each layer.

Application Layer

The Application layer communicates with other computers using: *FTP, TFTP, HTTP, Telnet, SMTP gateways, SNMP, and DNS.* These protocols' features include:

- **FTP: The File Transfer Protocol (FTP)** *uses a reliable connection to send, delete, and move files to and from a FTP client and server. *Cisco routers do not support FTP, but do support TFTP.*

- **TFTP: The Trivial File Transfer Protocol (TFTP)** is similar to FTP, but is faster and less reliable because it uses an unreliable connection.

- **HTTP: The Hypertext Transfer Protocol (HTTP)** allows you to connect your computer to other computers on the Internet.

- **Telnet:** This is a terminal emulation protocol that allows you to log onto remote machines or telnet servers. Telnet is what you use to troubleshoot routers. This is a key utility, especially if your network has many routers. Note: If you are having network problems, Telnet uses each layer of OSI and is a good way to test each layer.

- **SMTP:** The Simple Mail Transfer Protocol (SMTP) is the e-mail transfer protocol. This protocol is responsible for transferring mail on TCP/IP networks and the Internet.

- **SNMP:** The Simple Network Management Protocol (SNMP) is used in TCP/IP networks for remote tracking and management. For example, SNMP hosts can report statistics such as hard drive space, network statistics, and other performance data to the administrator.

- **DNS:** The Domain Name System (DNS) service provides TCP/IP hostname to IP address resolution. For example, when you type a website's name into a web browser, the name must be resolved to an IP address before communication can take place. When setting up a workstation to access a DNS server you must have the following items: a domain, an IP address for the DNS server, or a host file.

In the Application layer you will find e-mail, file transfer, remote access, network management activities, client/server processes, name management, and information location. The Application layer involves user interaction with the computer and the network. This layer does not have its own protocols, but uses actual applications that the user will use.

Presentation Layer

The Presentation layer is *used to define data formats, encryption, data presentation, compression, and translation services.* The following perform functions at this layer:

- *TIFF
- GIF
- JPEG

- ASCII
- MPEG
- MIDI

- PICT
- ASN.1
- QuickTime

NOTE: ASN.1 is the standard data syntax used by the Presentation layer. MPEG is the standard for compression and coding of motion videos for CDs. TIFF is the standard graphics format used for high-resolution bitmapped images.

This layer defines how the data will be presented to the Application layer. In other words, this layer prepares the data from the Application layer for transmission over the network. It also reformats data received from the lower layers for the Application layer.

Session Layer

The Session layer *defines how to start, control, and end conversations (dialog control)*. It uses *RPC, NFS, SQL, NetBIOS Names, X Windows, AppleTalk ASP, and DECnet SCP.*

NOTE: X Windows is used by intelligent terminals for communication with Unix computers.

This layer allows two applications to have a conversation or dialog. *At this layer, sessions between network stations are established, managed, and terminated*. It also keeps different applications' data separate. *Checkpoints are a function of this layer.* This layer is responsible for:

- Establishing a connection
- Maintaining the session

- Ending the session
- Dialog separation

- Dialog control

The Session layer coordinates communication between systems and organizes their communication by three different modes:

- **Simplex mode:** Communication is actually a monologue with one device transmitting and another receiving.

- **Half-duplex mode:** Nodes take turns transmitting and receiving.

- **Full-duplex mode:** Both sides transmit and receive simultaneously.

NOTE: You will see more on duplexing later on.

The Upper Layers

Table 1-1 lists the responsibilities of each of the upper layers.

Table 1-1: The Upper Layers

Layer	Responsibility
Application	Provides the user interface. Provides services to applications. Initiates the request for network services.
Presentation	Presents data. Defines data formats, encryption, compression, and translation services.
Session	Failure recovery. Data synchronization. Control for data exchange (full- or half-duplex).

These are the areas that are generally testable on the CCNA examination:

1. Describe flow control and how it is used within a network.

2. Understand how the Transport layer flow control mechanism works.

3. Connection-oriented and connectionless protocols:

   - Describe connection-oriented and connectionless network services and identify the key differences between them.

   - Define flow control and describe the three basic models used in networking.

Transport Layer

Transport-layer functions include flow control, multiplexing, virtual circuit management, and error checking and recovery. This layer uses checksums to determine if a packet arrives without error. It also provides for end-to-end connection. The following protocols operate at the Transport layer:

- *TCP*
- *UDP*
- *SPX*
- *ATP*

Services performed in this layer segment and reassemble data from upper-layer applications and then place it onto the same data stream. *The Transport layer provides end-to-end data transport service. It also establishes a logical connection between two hosts.* Data integrity is guaranteed at this layer with flow control (UDP does not do this). Flow control prevents the sending host on one side of the connection from overflowing the buffers in the receiving host. Overflow can result in lost and unreliable data. Reliable data transport uses a connection-oriented communication session between two hosts.

Connection-oriented communication uses error recovery (TCP or SPX) or pre-established pathing. In reliable communications, one device first establishes a connection-oriented session with another device. The two devices communicate with each other by sending messages over the network confirming that the transfer is approved and that both sides are ready for it to take place. After this confirmation is complete, a connection is established and the data transfer can start.

This process is sometimes called a three-way handshake. Even as the data is being transferred between hosts, the two devices check with each other to ensure that the data is being transferred properly.

Protocols that use error recovery are considered to be connection-oriented. They must first agree to create a connection. The sender of data then waits for an acknowledgment that the receiver of the data has indeed received the data. To qualify as connection-oriented, the protocol must have error recovery or pre-established pathing. **Pre-established pathing** hides the details of any network-dependent information from the upper layers by providing transparent data transfer.

Connectionless: Uses simple delivery of data, with no error recovery or pre-established pathing (IPX, UDP, IP).

Connection-oriented protocols (TCP): Uses flow control to control the rate at which data is sent to another computer. Flow control is needed because a computer can sometimes send data faster than the receiving computer can store it in its buffers. Data arriving without corruption is controlled at the Transport layer by maintaining flow control. Reliable data transport uses connection-oriented communication sessions. The protocol then ensures the following will be achieved:

- The segments received are acknowledged back to the sender.

- Any segments not acknowledged are retransmitted.

- Segments are sequenced back into their proper order at the receiving device.

- Flow control is used to avoid congestion, overloading, and data loss.

The three methods for handling network congestion are:

Buffering: Computers have limited buffer space to hold incoming data in memory until processed. Infrequent bursts of data are no problem and can be handled by buffering. When data bursts become more frequent they can use up the remaining memory, and the device will have no choice but to discard any additional datagrams that arrive.

Source-quench Messages: These are used by the receiving devices to assist in preventing the buffers from overflowing. The receiving device sends source-quench messages to tell the source to reduce its current rate of data transmission. In other words, stop transmitting until it can clear out the buffers.

Windowing: The amount of data transmitted would be low if the transmitting machine had to wait for an acknowledgment after each segment. The number of data segments the transmitting machine is allowed to send without receiving an acknowledgment for each is called a window. Windowing is the number of packets that the two devices agree to send before an acknowledgment is sent.

These are the areas that are generally testable on the CCNA examination:

Examination of OSI layer-3 (networking) functions:

- Identify and describe the functions of the Network layer.

- Describe data link addresses and network addresses, and identify the key differences between them.

- List the key internetworking functions of the Network layer and describe how they are performed in a router.

- Describe the two parts of network addressing, then identify the parts in specific protocol address examples.

Network Layer

The two major functions of the Network layer are end-to-end routing and addressing. This means that the Network layer is responsible for transporting data between devices that are not locally (directly) attached. *Routers (layer-3 devices) operate at this layer.* The Network layer performs the function of addressing and the delivery of packets, sometimes called datagrams. The router is a device that determines the best path to send a packet based on cost and network layer information. Here is something interesting: If Host A sends a packet to Host B over Ethernet and Host B is not active, the packet will time out.

The Network

The following are the three steps of routing:

- Send the data from the source computer. This is the computer that is sending the data.

- Transfer the data from the source to its nearest router, then to a router that supports the receiving device.

- Deliver the data from the router that supports the receiving device to the host on the local network. This is the computer that you send the data to.

Network layer addressing:

- ***Network layer addresses are created to allow logical grouping of addresses.*** Logical addressing means that the devices do not have to be located in the same physical area. In a nutshell, logical addressing is used to send data to a different network or, as we will discuss later, a different subnet. In TCP/IP the group is called a network or subnet, while in IPX it is only called a network. (I will discuss physical addressing using MAC addresses in the Data Link layer.)

- Network layer addresses are also grouped on physical location in a local network that has subnets. If you don't have subnets, a router is not necessary and therefore not used. Routing is based on the fact that addresses are grouped together in another network or subnet. The routing table entry for each network will reference the group (network or subnet), but not each individual address. In other words, when routing is performed it is done based on the network portion of the IP address and does not even consider the host portion. Then, when the packet reaches the router responsible for supporting that network, the data is delivered using the receiving host's MAC address. (It took me a long time to realize that the IP address is not used to deliver the data to its end destination.)

- A network address consists of two parts: the network portion and the host portion. As you look at the chart you may wonder why IP can have a range of bits for the network and host portions. Well, that is because it allows for the three classes (Class A, B, C) as well as subnetting. (We will cover subnetting later.) Table 1-2 shows some protocols broken down by network and host.

Table 1-2: Protocols

Protocol	Total Bits	Network Portion	Host Portion
*IP	32 BITS	(8-30 BITS) NETWORK	(2-24 BITS) HOST
*IPX	80 BITS	(32 BITS) NETWORK	(48 BITS) NODE
AppleTalk	24 BITS	(16 BITS) NETWORK	(8 BITS) NODE

EXAM TIP: You need to know that IP is made up of 32 bits and IPX is made up of 80 bits. Also notice that the IPX network portion is always 32 bits and the node potion is always 48 bits (the MAC address). *IP addresses have a total of 32 bits. The network portion can range from 8-30 bits because of the 3 classes (A, B, and C). The host portion can range from 2-24 bits.

Routing Terms

Routing protocols: Routing tables are built dynamically by the use of a routing protocol. Examples are RIP and IGRP, to be discussed later.

Routed protocols: These are the ones being routed (IP, IPX).

Routing table: This is where the information needed to perform routing is held.

Summary: The routing table is where the information needed to perform routing is held, as built by the routing protocol. It is used by the routing process to forward the packets of the routed protocol.

EXAM TIP: You need to be able to recognize an IP address and an IPX address when you see them. You also have to be able to identify the network and host portion of each. Finally, be able to identify what routing and routed protocols do. Here is a sample IP address: 172.10.20.4. Now the IPX address: 4a.0000.6789.4321. Notice that the network address for the IP address is 172.10 and the host portion is 20.4. The network address for the IPX address is 4a and the host portion is what's left. By the way, the rest is the MAC address of the NIC card.

The Network Layer in Detail

The Network layer defines end-to-end delivery of packets, uses logical addressing, and defines how routing works. It uses *IP, IPX.* This layer supports both connection-oriented and connectionless service from the Transport layer protocols. Networking layer protocols include routing protocols, which are IP and IPX. The most common routing protocols are: Border Gateway Protocol (BGP), Open Shortest Path First (OSPF), and Routing Information Protocol (RIP).

Routers use the Network layer to send data. Sending packets from the source network (router) to the destination network (router) is the Network layer's primary function. After the router decides on the best path to take it will start the delivery process. This is known as packet switching. The router forwards the packet received by the router on one network interface to the port that connects to the best path through the network. That port will then send the packet to the addressee of that packet. *The Network layer process examines the packet's header to discover which network the packet is addressed to.* It then uses the routing table to find the network that the packet is addressed to.

After a route is selected, the packet is re-encapsulated into a data link frame with the selected hardware address information (for the supporting router) and sends it to the next hop in the path toward its destination. This process is repeated every time the packet switches to another router. When the packet finally reaches the router that supports the receiving host, it is encapsulated in the destination LAN's data link frame type and delivered to the intended host. Isn't that strange? IP is used even less than you probably thought. In essence, the IP address doesn't deliver data; it is just used to identify a network, and data link kicks in using hardware addresses (MAC addresses).

Two types of packets are seen in the Network layer: the actual data and route updates.

- Data packets transport user data throughout the network. The protocols used to support data traffic are called routed protocols.

- A router uses route update packets to update neighboring routers about its network connections to other routers in the network.

*Routers break up broadcast domains. This means that broadcasts are not forwarded through a router. Routers also break up collision domains. (*layer-2 switches also break up collision domains, but not broadcast domains.)* It is important to note that hubs, repeaters, bridges, and switches will forward broadcast packets. Each interface on a router is a separate network and must be assigned a unique network identification, which is the network portion of the address. Each host on the network connected to that router interface must use that same network address number.

Some major points about routers are:

- Routers do not forward broadcast or multicast packets. (Bridges do forward these types of packets.)

- Routers use the logical address (IP address) to determine the next hop router that will be used to forward the packet.

- Routers use access lists to control security of packets trying to enter or exit an interface.

- Routers can provide layer-2 bridging functions if needed.

- Layer-3 devices (switches and routers) provide connections between virtual LANs.

These are the areas that are generally testable on the CCNA examination:

1. Examination of Data-Link functions:

   - Identify and describe the functions of the Data Link layer.

   - Describe data link addresses and network addresses and identify the key differences between them.

   - Define and describe the functions of a MAC address.

2. Define and explain the five conversion steps of data encapsulation.

Data Link Layer

The Data Link layer includes physical addressing, error notification, sequencing of frames, and flow control. This layer is the delivery mechanism that delivers data across a particular link by using its hardware address. This layer uses *HDLC, frame relay, PPP, and IEEE 802.3/802.2*.

The Data Link layer makes sure that messages are delivered to the proper physical device. It also translates information from the Network layer and converts it to frames for the Physical layer to process. More precisely, it formats the information into *data frames* and adds a customized header containing the hardware destination and hardware source address. A host sends data to individual hosts and between routers using the Data Link layer hardware address. As a packet is sent between routers, it is framed with information at the Data Link layer, but that information is stripped off at the receiving router and the original IP packet is left completely intact.

Logical Link Control (LLC) Sublayer: This sublayer operates between the Network layer and the MAC sublayer of the Data Link layer. LLC allows protocols at the Network layer, like IP, to operate without being concerned with what's happening at the Physical layer. This sublayer is also responsible for timing and flow control.

Media Access Control (MAC) Sublayer: The MAC sublayer of the Data Link layer is responsible for framing. This sublayer makes frames from the 1s and 0s that the Physical layer receives from the wire, which is a digital signal. This layer first checks the CRC to make sure that the data was not damaged in transit. It then checks to make sure the hardware address matches. The MAC sublayer is also responsible for media access using a NIC and the network card driver.

The MAC (Media Access Control) address (sometimes called Ethernet address, physical address, and NIC address) is assigned by the manufacturer and is burned into a ROM or EEPROM on the NIC.

EXAM TIP: Memorize the protocols used at the Data Link layer and the services that this layer provides. The services are physical addressing, error notification, sequencing of frames, and flow control. Additionally, you need to know that LLC and MAC are sublayers of the Data Link layer.

WAN Protocols at the Data Link layer: These define how frames are carried between devices on a single data link. The most used encapsulations for synchronous serial lines are:

- **High-Level Data Link Control (HDLC):** Created to support both multipoint and point-to-point configurations. *HDLC is the Cisco default protocol for all serial links, and it can't communicate over a serial link with another vendor's HDLC protocol.* HDLC was derived from SDLC.

- **Synchronous Data Link Control (SDLC):** A protocol created by IBM to make it easier for their mainframes to connect to remote offices.

- **Link Access Procedure, Balanced (LAPB):** Created to be used with X.25. LAPB can detect out-of-sequence or missing frames. It can also retransmit, exchange, and acknowledge frames.

- **X.25:** Defines the point-to-point communication between Data Terminal Equipment (DTE) and Data Circuit-terminating Equipment (DCE).

- **Serial Line IP (SLIP):** The industry standard developed in 1984 to support TCP/IP networking over low-speed serial interfaces.

- **Point-to-Point Protocol (PPP):** This protocol uses the specifications of SLIP and makes it better by adding login, password, and error correction capabilities. PPP can be used with IP, IPX, and AppleTalk.

- **Integrated Services Digital Network (ISDN):** This operates through analog phone lines converted to use digital signaling. PPP uses tunneling, which is the process in which frames from one network system are placed inside the frames of another network system. With ISDN you can transmit both voice and data.

- **Frame Relay:** An upgraded version of X.25 to be used where LAPB is no longer utilized. It's the fastest of the WAN protocols, because of its simplified framing approach, and has no error correction. It needs high-quality digital phone lines and may not be available in some locations.

EXAM TIP: Remember that HDLC must be used for all serial links. If it is not used communications will not happen.

Physical Layer

The Physical layer defines the type of cable and connectors. This layer has two responsibilities: It sends bits and receives bits. This layer defines the interface between the Data Terminal Equipment (DTE) and the Data Circuit-terminating Equipment (DCE). *The DCE is usually located at the service provider, while the DTE is the attached device. The services available to the DTE are most often accessed via a modem or channel service unit/data service unit (CSU/DSU).*

Hubs, which are really multiple port repeaters, operate here.

The standards at the Physical layer are:

- *EIA/TIA-232*
- *EIA/TIA-449*
- *V.24*
- *V.35*
- *X.21*
- *G.703*
- *EIA-530*

The Lower Layers

Table 1-3 lists the responsibilities of each of the lower layers.

Table 1-3: The Lower Layers

Layer	Responsibility
Transport	Segments and reassembles data. Provides end-to-end data transport. Establishes a logical connection. Uses flow control. Uses acknowledgments and retransmission.
Network	Provides end-to-end routing. Uses logical addressing.
Data Link	Uses physical addressing (MAC). Performs error notification. Sequences frames and flow control.
Physical	Defines type of cable. Sends bits and receives bits.

EXAM TIP: Memorize Table 1-3 to prepare yourself for the exam.

Data Encapsulation: This process places data between headers and trailers for each OSI layer. Each layer encapsulates the data from the layer above it as the data flows down the protocol stack. Starting at the Application layer, data is encapsulated in Presentation layer information. The Presentation layer sends the data to the Session layer that's responsible for synchronizing the session with the destination host. The Session layer gives this data to the Transport layer, which transports the data from the source host to the destination host. But before this happens, the Network layer adds routing information to the packet. The packet is then passed to the Data Link layer for framing and for connection to the Physical layer. The Physical layer sends the data as 1s and 0s to the destination host across the media.

Table 1-4 depicts an easy way to memorize the process:

Table 1-4: Data Encapsulation Steps

The Five Steps of Data Encapsulation	
User information is converted to data.	*Application*
Data is converted to segments.	*Transport*
Segments are converted to packets or datagrams.	*Network*
Packets or datagrams are converted to frames.	*Data Link*
Frames are converted to bits.	*Physical*

EXAM TIP: Learn Table 1-4 to tell what happens at each layer.

Broadcast: This is a frame sent to all network nodes at the same time. A broadcast tells all the hosts on the network to receive it and process the data. This can be both positive and negative for network performance. For example, if a server needs to send data to all the hosts on the network segment, network broadcasts can be good. However, if there are too many broadcasts on the network segment, network performance can be negatively impacted. That is why it is important to segment your network properly with bridges and/or routers.

CISCO THREE-LAYER MODEL

The Three-Layer Model is a Cisco model to help you design, implement, and maintain a network. Figure 1-2 illustrates the three-layer hierarchical model.

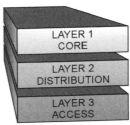

LAYER 1
CORE

LAYER 2
DISTRIBUTION

LAYER 3
ACCESS

Figure 1-2: Cisco Three-Layer Model

Chapter 1

The Core Layer

The Core layer is at the top of the model, and is responsible for transporting large amounts of traffic reliably and quickly. The primary purpose of the Core layer is to switch traffic as fast as possible. User data is processed at the Distribution layer, which forwards requests to the core if needed. If there is a failure in the core, all users will more than likely be affected. You must provide fault tolerance at this layer.

Don'ts at the core:

- Don't do anything to slow down traffic. For example, don't use access lists and don't route between virtual local area networks. Additionally, don't use packet filtering.

- Don't provide workgroup support in this layer. Don't expand the core when the network grows (adding routers). Upgrade devices before you decide to add devices.

Do's at the core:

- Design the core for high reliability. Try using data-link technologies that increase speed and redundancy, such as Fast Ethernet.

- Choose routing protocols with the lowest convergence times. Your routing table must be current and up to date in order for your network to perform at its best.

The Distribution Layer

The Distribution layer is usually called the workgroup layer. The primary function of this layer is to provide routing, filtering, and WAN access. It is also responsible for determining how packets will access the core. This layer must use the fastest means that network service requests are handled. Several things should be done at the Distribution layer:

- Use access lists and packet filtering.

- Use security and network policies like firewalls.

- Static routing.

- Routing between VLANs is performed at this layer.

The Access Layer

The Access layer is where user and workgroup access to internetwork resources is controlled. It also handles traffic for remote services. Some things that are to be considered at this layer include:

- Creation of separate collisions domains (segmentation).
- Workgroup connectivity into the Distribution layer.
- Ethernet switching and static routing (instead of dynamic routing).

EXAM TIP: The exam has not previously addressed these areas, but questions could come from here sometime in the future.

TOPOLOGIES

Figure 1-3 illustrates the star, bus, ring, and mesh networks.

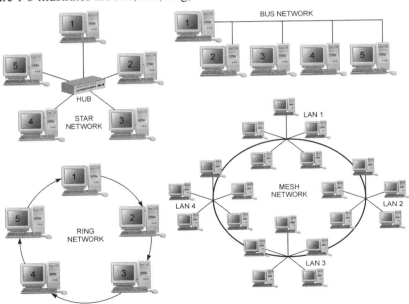

Figure 1-3: The Star, Bus, Ring, and Mesh Networks

The following is a quick overview of the most common types of networks:

- **Bus:** All devices are connected to a common shared cable (backbone). This type of network uses Carrier Sense Multiple Access with Collision Detection (CSMA/CD), which means that all the devices on the network can transmit at the same time and provide collision detection in the event that two computers try to send data at the same time.

- **Ring:** Devices are usually wired in a physical circle. Each node is connected to its neighbors on either side, and data passes around the ring in one direction.

- **Star:** Requires that all devices connect to a central hub, and usually uses CSMA/CD. Hubs employ shared Ethernet, which is a half-duplex method of transmitting and receiving. Switched Ethernet uses full-duplex to eliminate collisions. Because half-duplex operation is required for CSMA/CD, full-duplex is not possible with a 10BASE-T hub. Full-duplex operates with the CSMA/CD circuit disabled. Full-duplex eliminates contention (devices competing for media access) on point-to-point links. Full-duplex Ethernet has both loopback and collision detection disabled.

- **Mesh:** An all-channel topology in which each device is directly connected to every other device on the network, providing redundancy.

- **FDDI (Fiber Data Distributed Interface):** Developed in the mid-1980s by ANSI (American National Standards Institute) to address the growing needs for bandwidth. FDDI does not use full-duplex. Ethernet over fiber is 100BASE-FX. Fiber has some advantages over copper wire:

  - Immunity to electrical interference

  - Much higher throughput

  - Immunity to traditional wiretap methods

  - Capacity over much longer distances

- **Token Ring (802.5) network:** Created by IBM in the 1970s, a token-passing network connects the rings in a logical ring topology. Token passing uses a small, specially formatted frame, called a token, which is passed from node to node on the ring. The Token Ring specification is nearly identical to the IEEE 802.5 specification. Token Ring stations are connected together by a MSAU (Multi-Station Access Unit). If a transmitting station fails, the active monitor removes the token.

- **Ethernet:** Usually referred to as *10BASE-T, which can have up to 100-meter segments*. It was created by Digital, Intel, and Xerox (collectively known as DIX) in the 1970s. Ethernet employs CSMA/CD (Carrier Sense Multiple Access with Collision Detection). Nodes can access the network any time they have data to send. Before a node transmits data, it "listens" to the wire to see if the network is busy. If it is not, it transmits. Collisions occur if two nodes listen, hear nothing, and transmit simultaneously. This ruins both transmissions. ***There is a back-off algorithm that creates a random wait time for retransmission so that a second collision does not occur.***

- Ethernet commonly uses RJ-45 connectors at the hardware layer.

- Fast Ethernet employs auto-negotiation, which allows an Ethernet device to determine the speed of the link and the duplex (half or full) setting. Auto-negotiation has been known to fail. Cisco recommends using static settings for important devices.

- **UTP (Unshielded Twisted Pair):** This is the cable generally used in Ethernet networks. These wires are unshielded because UTP derives all of its EMI protection from the cancellation effect of twisted pairs. This technique minimizes the absorption of EMI from the surrounding environment, helping reduce cross talk and nearby electrical noise.

- **STP (Shielded Twisted Pair):** This is similar to UTP, but has a foil shield covering the wires to reduce EMI. IEEE 802.3 10Base2 standard (called thin net) uses BNC T-connectors for connecting computers to cables. This standard is not seen much anymore because of the cost of the cabling.

Review Questions

1. File, print, message, database, and application services take place at which OSI layer?
    a. Application
    b. Presentation
    c. Session
    d. Transportation

2. Which of the following is the standard data syntax used by the Presentation layer?
    a. JPEG
    b. MIDI
    c. ASN.1
    d. SMTP

3. Which of the following is the standard for compression and coding of motion video for CDs?
    a. ASN.1
    b. MPEG
    c. TIFF
    d. JPEG

4. Which of the following is the standard graphics format used for high-resolution bitmapped images?
    a. QuickTime
    b. ASCII
    c. GIF
    d. TIFF

5. Select all the following standards or protocols that perform functions within the Presentation layer of the OSI model.
    a. FTP
    b. PICT
    c. SQL
    d. TIFF
    e. RPC
    f. JPEG

6. Encryption, compression, and translation take place at which OSI layer?
    a. Presentation
    b. Session
    c. Application
    d. Transport

7. Checkpoints are a function of which OSI layer?
    a. Presentation
    b. Session
    c. Application
    d. Transport

8. Select all the following standards or protocols that perform functions within the Session layer of the OSI model.
   a. SQL
   b. RPC
   c. MIDI
   d. Telnet
   e. TIFF
   f. X Windows

9. Select all the following standards or protocols that perform functions within the Session layer of the OSI model.
   a. ASN.1
   b. ASCII
   c. SMTP
   d. NFS
   e. ASP
   f. DECnet SCP

10. Which of the following is used by intelligent terminals for communicating with Unix computers?
    a. RPC
    b. NFS
    c. X Windows
    d. ASP
    e. DECnet SCP

11. Which of the following are Transport layer protocols? (Select all that apply.)
    a. UDP
    b. TCP
    c. ATP
    d. SPX
    e. All of the above

12. At the receiving computer, reassembling the packets in the proper sequence is the responsibility of which OSI layer?
    a. Transport
    b. Network
    c. Session
    d. Data Link

13. Windowing is a function of which OSI layer?
    a. Session
    b. Data Link
    c. Network
    d. Transport

14. Regulating the amount of data sent from the source computer to the destination computer is a function of which OSI layer?
    a. Transport
    b. Network
    c. Data Link
    d. Session

15. Routers can provide which of the following functions? (Select all that apply.)
    a. Breakup of collision domains
    b. Decrease of collision domains
    c. Breakup of broadcast domains
    d. Decrease of broadcast domains
    e. Logical network addressing
    f. Physical addressing
    g. Physical address filtering of the local network

16. What are the two sublayers in the Data Link layer?
    a. LLC
    b. MAC
    c. Data Link
    d. Physical
    e. IP

17. Framing takes place at which OSI layer?
    a. Transport
    b. Network
    c. Data Link
    d. Physical

18. The following services are performed within various layers of the OSI model:

   (1) Hides the details of any network-dependent information from the higher layers by providing transparent data transfer.

   (2) Formats the message into data frames and adds a customized header containing the hardware destination and a source address.

   (3) Decides on the best path to send packets out across the network.

   Select the correct order (1,2,3) that describes the OSI layer functions depicted above:
   a. Transport, Data Link, Network
   b. Data Link, Network, Transport
   c. Network, Data Link, Transport
   d. Transport, Network, Data Link

19. Which of the following is true when a broadcast is sent in an Ethernet LAN?
   a. All devices receive it and process it.
   b. Only the destination device receives it and processes it.
   c. Broadcasts are transmitted through a router.
   d. Broadcasts are not transmitted through a bridge.

1. **a.** In the Application layer you will find e-mail, file transfer, remote access, network management activities, client/server processes, name management, and information location.

2. **c.** ASN.1 is the standard data syntax used by the Presentation layer.

3. **b.** MPEG is the standard for compression and coding of motion videos for CDs.

4. **d.** TIFF is the standard graphics format used for high-resolution bitmapped images.

5. **b, d, f.** PICT, TIFF, JPEG, GIF, MPEG, MIDI, QuickTime, ASCII, and ASN.1 are standards or protocols that perform functions at the Presentation layer.

6. **a.** The Presentation layer is used to define data formats, encryption, compression, and translation services.

7. **b.** Checkpoints are a function of the Session layer.

8. **a, b, f.** The Session layer defines how to start, control, and end conversations (dialog control). It uses RPC, NFS, SQL, NetBIOS Names, X Window, AppleTalk ASP, and DECnet SCP.

9. **d, e, f.** The Session layer defines how to start, control, and end conversations (dialog control). It uses RPC, NFS, SQL, NetBIOS Names, X Windows, AppleTalk ASP, and DECnet SCP.

10. **c.** X Windows is used by intelligent terminals for communication with Unix computers.

11. **e.** Transport-layer functions include flow control, multiplexing, virtual circuit management, and error checking and recovery. It also provides for end-to-end connection. It uses UDP, TCP, ATP, and SPX.

12. **a.** Data arriving without corruption is controlled at the Transport layer by maintaining flow control.

13. **d.** Windowing is one of three methods for handling network congestion in the Transport layer. The amount of data transmitted would be low if the transmitting machine had to wait for an acknowledgment after each segment. The number of data segments the transmitting machine is allowed to send without receiving an acknowledgment for each is called a window. Windowing is the number of packets that the two devices agree to send before an acknowledgment is sent.

14. **a.** Flow control is used to control the rate at which data is sent to another computer. Flow control is needed because a computer can sometimes send data faster than the receiving computer can store it in its buffers. Data arriving without corruption is controlled at the Transport layer by maintaining flow control.

15. **a, c, e, g.** Routers break up broadcast domains. This means that broadcasts are not forwarded through a router. Routers also break up collision domains. They use the logical address (IP address) to determine the next hop that will be used to forward the packet. Routing is performed based on the fact that addresses are grouped together on physical location in a local network or subnet, using the network portion of the IP address.

16. **a, b.** The Logical Link Control (LLC) sublayer operates between the Network layer and the MAC sublayer of the Data Link layer. LLC allows protocols at the Network layer to operate without being concerned with what's happening at the Physical layer. The Media Access Control (MAC) sublayer of the Data Link layer is responsible for framing. The MAC sublayer is also responsible for media access using a NIC and the network card driver.

17. **c.** The MAC sublayer of the Data Link layer is responsible for framing.

18. **a.** The Transport layer uses pre-established pathing to hide the details of any network-dependent information from the upper layers by providing transparent data transfer. The Data Link layer formats the information into data frames and adds a customized header containing the hardware destination and hardware source address. Routers use the Network layer to send data. The Network layer's primary function is sending packets from the source network (router) to the destination network (router). After the router decides on the best path to take it will start the delivery process.

19. **a.** A broadcast (frame) is sent to all network nodes at the same time. A broadcast tells all the hosts on the network to receive it and process the data.

Chapter 2

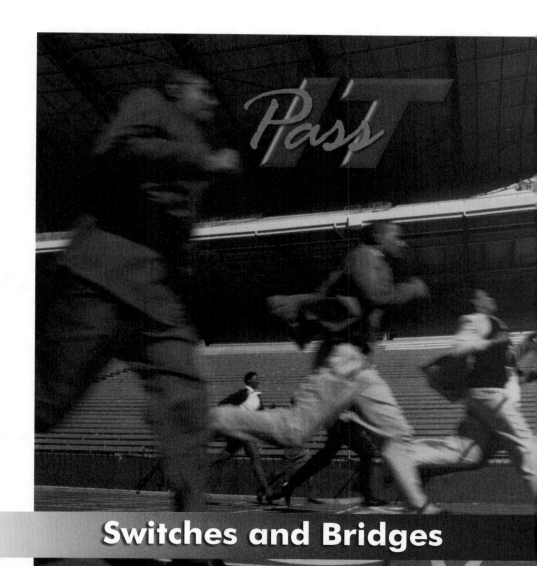

Switches and Bridges

These are the areas that are generally testable on the CCNA examination:

1. Describe layer-2 switching.

2. Describe address learning in layer-2 switches.

3. Understand when a layer-2 switch will forward or filter a frame.

4. Describe network loop problems in layer-2 switched networks.

5. Describe the Spanning-Tree Protocol.

6. List the LAN switch types and describe how they work with layer-2 switches.

Introduction

Chapter 2 is one of the most important chapters in this book, because Cisco really emphasizes switches and bridges on the exam. We will start out with relieving network congestion through various methods.

Then we'll move on to the three switch functions at layer 2 (Data Link), which are address learning, forward/filtering, and loop avoidance. Next is Ethernet congestion and some of the most common problems associated with it. Then I'll cover ways to reduce or eliminate this congestion. You will learn the positive and negative aspects of each method.

The next section on the three switching modes is important. I will give you the traits of each mode as this area is covered extensively on the exam. A word to the wise — know the differences between these types of switching.

Finally, you will learn how the Spanning-Tree Protocol works and all the information you need to prepare for the exam.

HOW TO RELIEVE NETWORK CONGESTION

It's a good idea to segment your network with bridges and routers when your network starts to grow too big. Use these methods:

- **Physical segmentation:** *You can segment the network with bridges and routers, thereby breaking up the collision domains. *Bridged networks break up collision domains, but the network is still one large broadcast domain.*

- **Full-duplex Ethernet devices:** *These can provide almost twice the bandwidth, but the NIC must be able to run in full-duplex mode.*

- **Network switching technology:** Switches can also be used for LAN segmentation. LAN switches provide dedicated, point-to-point, packet-switched connections between their ports.

- **Fast Ethernet:** Using Fast Ethernet switches can give you 10 times the amount of normal bandwidth.

Three Switch Functions at Layer 2

- **Address learning:** Layer-2 switches and bridges remember the source hardware address of each frame received on an interface and put this information into a MAC database. The next time a frame enters that interface, the MAC database is used to quickly send the data to its destination.

    - The MAC filtering table is empty when a switch is first powered on. When the frame arrives at the switch the source address is placed into the MAC filtering table. The device makes a record, allowing it to remember which interface will be used. The switch then **floods** the network with this frame because it does not know where the destination address is located. When the device answers back, the switch takes the source address from that frame and places it into the MAC address database. From this point forward, the switch has two MAC address entries in the filtering table and can make a point-to-point connection. This means the frame will only be forwarded between the two devices, saving network bandwidth because the switch does not have to flood the network to learn an address.

- **Forward/filter decisions:** When a frame arrives at a switch interface, the destination hardware address is compared to the forward/filter MAC database. If the destination hardware address is listed in the MAC database and is part of this segment, it is only sent out to that addressee. The switch does not transmit the frame out to any other address. This "frame filtering" saves bandwidth on the other network segments.

- **Loop avoidance:** If you have multiple connections between switches, network loops can occur. *The Spanning-Tree Protocol (STP) is used to stop network loops and allow redundancy.*

The above switch functions increase available bandwidth on the network. Address learning keeps track of source addresses and sends the packet directly to the host, so there is no need for a broadcast that can increase traffic and reduce bandwidth. With forward/filter, if the host is on the same segment, the frame is only sent to the host, thereby reducing traffic.

Finally, if the loops are removed through the use of STP, the bandwidth is increased because of reduced traffic.

EXAM TIP: You will be required to know how a bridge or a switch processes frames. Again, read carefully and then try to understand what is going on.

These are the areas that are generally testable on the CCNA examination:

Understanding LANs and LAN switching:

- Describe full- and half-duplex Ethernet operation.

- Describe network congestion problems in Ethernet Networks.

- Describe the features and benefits of Fast Ethernet.

- Describe the guidelines and distance limitations of Fast Ethernet.

- Define and describe the function of a MAC address.

MAC Addresses

MAC addresses are a physical addressing method used to identify the LAN interface cards (NICs) on Ethernet LANs. They are also called unicast or individual addresses. NICs are hardwired (called firmware) with an individual address by the manufacturer. This is the address used between two computers on the same segment. The first half of the address identifies the vendor; the second part is a unique number (serial number) that the vendor assigns to it. Switches use MAC addresses to filter packets and to determine the destination address.

Ethernet Congestion

Usually found in 10BASE-5 and 10BASE-2 topologies. The bus is shared between all the devices on the Ethernet, which use Carrier Sense Multiple Access/Collision Detection (CSMA/CD) to access the bus.

Collisions happen when two computers send data at the same time. Frames that collide need to be resent. Devices might have to wait to send a frame because another device is currently sending. *This is called a back-off, which is a random wait time for retransmission so that a second collision does not occur.*

Full-Duplex Ethernet

The use of full-duplex can relieve congestion considerably. Full-duplex uses 10BASE-T topology. This type of topology uses switches. So full-duplex can only occur in switches. *The "BASE" in 10BASE-T refers to the type of wire signaling rate used.*

In full-duplex, collisions are not possible, thus reducing Ethernet congestion. *Another benefit is that there is 10 Mbps bandwidth in each direction. (The bandwidth could be greater if you are using Fast Ethernet.) So if you have a 10BASE-T network running in full-duplex mode with 8 separate connections to a switch, what is the bandwidth of each connection? (Answer: 10 Mbps in each direction or 20 Mbps per connection)*

- **Full-Duplex Ethernet:** Can both transmit and receive simultaneously, but it requires a switch port, not a hub, to do this. It uses point-to-point connections and is usually collision-free since it doesn't share bandwidth with any other devices. Information sent by two devices cannot collide because there are two physically separate transmit and receive circuits between them.

In order to run full-duplex, you must have the following:

- Two 10 Mbps or 100 Mbps paths (on one cable)
- Full-duplex NIC cards
- Loopback and collision detection disabled
- Software drivers supporting two simultaneous data paths
- 10BASE-T/100BASE-T or 10BASE-FL/100BASE-FL

EXAM TIP: Expect to be tested on Ethernet congestion and full-duplex. Just remember the golden rule (actually my rule): Highlighted items mean "read and understand."

Half-Duplex Ethernet Design

Half-duplex is when one device can send to another device and the other device can do the same, but only one way at a time. *This uses a single cable and is similar to a narrow one-way bridge.*

100BASE-T Fast Ethernet

Also known as IEEE 802.3u, 100BASE-T Fast Ethernet uses the CSMA/CD protocol, and is 10 times faster than 10BASE-T. Cisco supports all of the 100BASE-T standards, except the *100VG AnyLan standard.*

Fast Ethernet

Runs at 100 Mbps, which is 10 times faster than 10BASE-T.

Two big features of Fast Ethernet are the faster speed and auto-negotiation. Auto-negotiation allows a NIC, hub, or switch to determine which type of 100 Mbps Ethernet is supported by the device on the other end of the cable. Support for half- or full-duplex is also negotiated. If the other device does not support auto-negotiation, auto-negotiation will settle for half-duplex 10BASE-T.

These are the areas that are generally testable on the CCNA examination:

Ethernet LAN segmentation:

- Describe the advantages of LAN segmentation.
- Describe LAN segmentation using bridges.
- Describe LAN segmentation using routers.
- Describe LAN segmentation using switches.
- Describe network congestion problems in Ethernet networks.
- Describe the benefits of network segmentation with bridges.
- Describe the benefits of network segmentation with routers.
- Describe the benefits of network segmentation with switches.

ETHERNET LAN SEGMENTATION

Ethernet LAN Segmentation Advantages

- *Decreases or eliminates collisions*
- *Increases the amount of total bandwidth per user*
- Confines user traffic to different LAN segments

LAN Segmentation with Bridges

Bridges learn MAC (or physical) addresses by examining the source MAC address of each frame that comes through the bridge. It then has to decide if the frame is to be forwarded or if the frame will be filtered. Basically, if the frame's destination is on the local segment, the frame will be sent to the addressee. If the frame's destination is not on the local segment, it is then filtered. Bridges create physically separate network segments to reduce traffic. They can dynamically build a forwarding table of information comprised of each MAC address and which segment that address is located on.

Bridges and switches, which are Data Link layer devices, are used to connect multiple network segments into a single logical network segment. What this means is that because these devices cannot segment the network like a router can, the network becomes a larger single broadcast network.

Attributes of bridging are the following:

- *Bridging uses MAC addressing, so installation is simple — no need for IP addresses*.
- *Collisions decrease because some frames are filtered*.
- *Bridges do not reduce the impact of broadcasts*.
- Total bandwidth is increased because each segment runs at 10 Mbps, not just a single large 10 Mbps segment.
- Traffic stays on the LAN segment if the destination address is on the same LAN.

- A drawback to using bridges is that if the destination MAC address is unknown to the bridge, the bridge will forward the frame to all segments.

EXAM TIP: It is important that you understand that bridges use MAC (physical) addressing and not IP (logical) addressing. Equally important is the fact that collision domains are decreased because some frames are filtered. Also, bridges do not reduce the impact of broadcasts — routers do.

LAN Segmentation Using Switches

A disadvantage of LAN segmentation using switches is that it *does not reduce broadcasts.*

Its benefits are as follows:

- Bandwidth is increased.

- Traffic stays on the segment for frames with the same source and destination address; switches filter some frames.

- Switches usually are optimized for speedy switching – *this is called wire speed*.

- It performs switching of frames using layer-2 (MAC) addresses, just like bridges.

EXAM TIP: Don't be confused about switches. They perform the same as bridges. They also do not reduce broadcast, but they do increase collision domains.

Bridging Instead of LAN Switching

Layer-2 switches are really just bridges with more ports, but there are some differences you should be aware of:

- Bridges are usually software-based, and switches are hardware-based because they use an Application-Specific Integrated Circuits (ASICs) chip to help make filtering decisions.

- Bridges can have only one spanning-tree instance per bridge, while switches can have many.

- Bridges can only have up to 16 ports, but a switch can have hundreds.

The greatest benefit of using switches instead of hubs in your network is that each switch port is its own collision domain, whereas a hub creates one large collision domain. However, switches and bridges do not break up broadcast domains.

Figure 2-1 illustrates a comparison between bridges and switches.

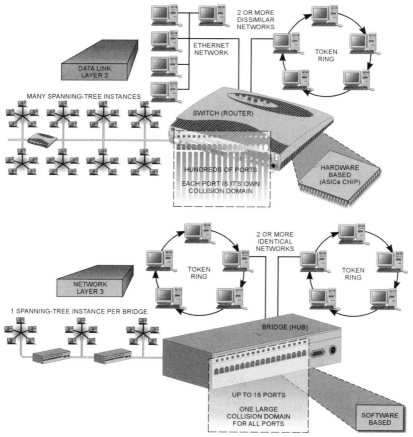

Figure 2-1: Comparison of Bridges and Switches

LAN Switching Modes

Store and Forward

Store and Forward waits to receive all bits in the frame (store) before forwarding the frame.

It *copies the entire frame into its onboard buffers and computes the cyclic redundancy check (CRC).* The frame is discarded if it contains a CRC error. If the frame doesn't contain errors, the LAN switch looks up the destination address in its table and forwards the frame. *Because it copies the entire frame, latency time can vary.* Depending on the size of the frame the time needed to process the frame will vary. This is the mode used by the Catalyst 5000 series switch and cannot be modified on the switch.

NOTE: The Store and Forward mode has the highest latency, because it waits to receive the entire frame, especially a large frame.

Cut Through

Cut Through reads the first bits in the destination address and the frame is sent before receiving the entire frame.

The LAN switch copies only the destination address (the first 6 bytes following the preamble) into its onboard buffers. It then looks up the destination address in its switching table and forwards the frame towards its destination. *A Cut Through switch provides reduced latency because it begins to forward the frame as soon as it reads the destination address.* Because it reduces latency, it is quicker than Store and Forward. However, there is a cost for the increased speed. The negative aspect is that a switch would still forward a collision frame or a frame with a bad CRC value. *Cut Through switching works at wire speed.*

NOTE: Cut Through has the lowest latency of all three modes because it sends the frame as soon as it reads the destination address.

Fragment Free

Fragment Free *performs like Cut Through, but waits for 64 bytes to be received before sending out the frame.*

Fragment Free is a modified form of Cut Through switching that waits for the collision window, which is 64 bytes long, to pass before forwarding. If a packet has an error, it usually occurs within the first 64 bytes. *64 bytes extends into the data portion (about 50% of the data) of the frame.* This is the default switching for the Catalyst 1900.

NOTE: Cut Through and Fragment Free have fixed latency times because each reads a predetermined portion of the frame before sending out the frame; Cut Through reads 6 bytes and Fragment Free reads 64 bytes.

Table 2-1 depicts the LAN switching modes.

Table 2-1: Switching Modes

Switching Type	Attributes
Store and Forward	Copies the entire frame into its onboard buffers and computes the cyclic redundancy check (CRC).
	Because it copies the entire frame, latency time can vary.
Cut Through	A Cut Through switch provides reduced latency because it begins to forward the frame as soon as it reads the destination address.
	Quicker than Store and Forward.
Fragment Free	Performs like Cut Through but waits for 64 bytes to be received before sending out the frame. 64 bytes extends into the data portion (about 50% of the data) of the frame.
	Slower than Cut Through, but provides for fault tolerance.
	Quicker than Store and Forward.

LAN Segmentation Using Routers

Routers use routing tables to make routing decisions. However, routers keep information in their tables only on how to get to remote networks, not to individual hosts. Key attributes include the following:

- *Broadcast frames are not forwarded by a router*.

- Routers deliver data at the Network layer (layer 3) by IP address (logical address).

- The router must process more of the frame to ensure delivery, which takes time. This means increased latency.

The Key Benefits of Segmentation with Routers

Routers provide a lower level of performance than bridges in relation to the number of frames or packets that can be processed in a given time frame. A router has to examine more information in a packet than a bridge, resulting in a 30-40% loss of throughput. Key benefits include the following:

- Manageability – Multiple routing protocols give the network manager more flexibility.

- Increased functionality – Routers provide features addressing the issues of flow, error, congestion control, reassembly, and control over packet lifetime.

- Collisions are decreased because frames between devices on the same segment are not forwarded by a router.

- Routers do not forward broadcasts.

- Multiple active paths (routes) are possible with routers.

NOTE: Because routers limit data to the segment it is intended for and broadcasts are not forwarded, routers create only one broadcast domain and one collision domain per segment.

SPANNING-TREE PROTOCOL

The purpose of the Spanning-Tree Protocol (STP) is to dynamically create a bridged/switched network in which only one path exists between any pair of LAN segments. It was developed to prevent routing loops in a network. If a switch has more than one path to the same destination, looping could occur. To prevent loops, the Spanning-Tree Protocol is used between the devices to detect and block redundant paths from the network. The STP will create a loop-free network. Figure 2-2 depicts a Spanning-Tree Protocol.

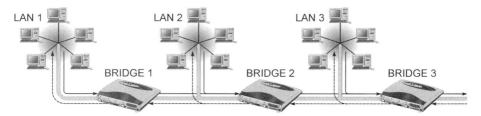

Figure 2-2: Spanning-Tree Protocol

The Spanning-Tree Protocol has frames called Bridge Protocol Data Units (BPDUs), which are sent and received by all switches in the network periodically. The frames aren't forwarded by the switches participating in the spanning tree, but are instead used to set up the spanning-tree topology itself. Catalyst 5000 series switches use IEEE 802.1d to perform this function.

Benefits include the following:

* Physically redundant paths in the network can exist and be used when other paths fail.

- Bridges, by default, are not capable of handling multiple active paths to the same MAC address. The Spanning-Tree Protocol prevents this by creating only one path.

- Loops in the bridged network are avoided.

How the Spanning-Tree Protocol Works

The Spanning-Tree Algorithm (STA) is used on each bridge interface by placing it into a forwarding state or a blocking state. Interfaces in the forwarding state are considered to be part of the spanning tree, while those in the blocking state are not.

Starting an Initial Spanning Tree

Initially, all bridges claim the root. They do this by sending their ID (MAC address) and priority. In the initial mode, all the bridges claim a priority of 0 (the highest), starting the selection process to identify which of the bridges is most capable of being in the spanning tree. To determine the root bridge, the priorities of the bridge and the MAC address are combined. If two switches or bridges have the same priority, then the MAC address is used to determine which one has the lowest ID.

Remember that the spanning-tree process causes some bridges to forward and others to block.

The spanning-tree process can recognize and then react to changes in the network topology. It does this with periodic notices sent to all the bridges. If there are no topology changes, meaning that there are no new bridges (to start an election), the notice is sent that there are no changes. Topology changes cause convergence when bridges and switches change to either the forwarding or blocking states. Convergence is the amount of time needed to notify all the bridges in the network of the topology changes. No data can be forwarded during this time. The problem with convergence is the time it takes for these devices to update. It usually takes 50 seconds to go from the blocking state to the forwarding state.

EXAM TIP: Primarily you need to know that the Spanning-Tree Protocol stops loops in bridges and switches. Read over the other information so you are familiar with the process.

Switches and Bridges

LAN DEVICES

Tables 2-2, 2-3, 2-4, and 2-5 list LAN devices that you need to be familiar with.

Table 2-2: Hubs

Does	Signal is transmitted to all other segments that are plugged into it.
Doesn't	Do not run in full-duplex mode.
Advantages	Connect all computer connections into one concentrator or device, price.
Responsibility	Can suffer latency. Cannot increase the number of collision or broadcast domains.

Table 2-3: Bridges

Does	Read the MAC or hardware address from the data frame, determine if the destination computer is on the local segment or on another network segment.
Doesn't	Do not forward the frame if destination computer is on the local segment.
Advantages	Can give more bandwidth than a repeater. Can increase the number of collision domains.
Responsibility	Can suffer from broadcast storms and latency. Cannot increase the number of broadcast domains.

Table 2-4: Routers

Does	Filter by both hardware (MAC) and network address (IP address), only forward packets to the network segment the packet is destined for.
Doesn't	N/A
Advantages	Prevent unnecessary network traffic. Can increase both collision and broadcast domains.
Responsibility	It takes a little more time to process frames.

Table 2-5: Switches

Does	Can run in half-duplex and full-duplex mode, read MAC address.
Doesn't	Do not route information using IP addressing.
Advantages	Send signal to the specific port where the destination MAC address is located. Can increase the number of collision domains.
Responsibility	Can suffer from broadcast storms and latency in half-duplex mode. Cannot increase the number of broadcast domains unless it is a VLAN.

Review Questions

1. Which form of duplexing uses a single cable and is analogous to a one-way bridge that allows traffic to go in both directions, but only one way at a time?
   a. Half-duplex
   b. Full-duplex
   c. Simplex
   d. Full- or half-duplex

2. Which of the following modes of switching has the highest latency?
    a. Cut Through
    b. Fragment Free
    c. Wire Speed
    d. Store and Forward

3. Which of the following modes of switching has the lowest latency?
    a. Cut Through
    b. Store and Forward
    c. Wire Speed
    d. Fragment Free

4. Which of the following modes of switching copies only the destination address into its buffers before forwarding?
    a. Fragment Free
    b. Wire Speed
    c. Cut Through
    d. Store and Forward

5. Which LAN switch methods have a fixed latency time? (Select two.)
    a. Store and Forward
    b. Cut Through
    c. Fragment Free
    d. Cut and Store

6. You have a LAN that is spread over two floors in a building. Lately the network has been slowing down. You put an analyzer on the network and notice that it has a very high number of broadcast packets. You would use which of the following to segment the network?
    a. Bridge
    b. Router
    c. Switch
    d. Repeater

7. You have 8 connections to a switch running 10 Mbps in full-duplex mode. What is the expected amount of data that each connection can use?
   a. 1.5 Mbps
   b. 20 Mbps
   c. 80 Mbps
   d. 100 Mbps

8. Which three basic switch functions increase available bandwidth on the network?
   a. Loop avoidance
   b. Address learning
   c. Packet forward/filtering
   d. All the above

9. Which of the following best describes how a bridge functions? (Select all that apply.)
   a. It maintains a table of IP addresses of the hosts it supports.
   b. It maintains a table of MAC addresses of the hosts it supports.
   c. It can create new collision domains.
   d. It can create new broadcast domains.

10. What are two purposes or attributes for segmentation with a bridge?
    a. Add a collision domain
    b. Reduce a collision domain
    c. Add a broadcast domain
    d. Increase bandwidth

11. What are the advantages of LAN segmentation with bridges?
    a. It decreases or eliminates collisions.
    b. It increases the amount of total bandwidth per user.
    c. It confines user traffic to different LAN segments.
    d. It will eliminate broadcasts.

12. Which of the following is true about the Fragment Free switch type?
    a. It reads 50% of the data before forwarding the frame.
    b. It reads all of the data before forwarding the frame.
    c. It only reads the destination address before forwarding the frame.
    d. It reads the entire frame before forwarding the frame.

13. Which of the following is a benefit of using routers to segment a network?
    a. It creates only one broadcast domain per segment.
    b. It creates only one collision domain per segment.
    c. It creates both one broadcast and collision domain per segment.
    d. None of the above

14. What is the purpose of the Spanning-Tree Protocol?
    a. To increase loops on the network
    b. To increase collision domains
    c. To decrease broadcast domains
    d. To maintain a loop-free network

15. What is the IEEE standard for the Spanning-Tree Protocol?
    a. IEEE 803.q
    b. IEEE 802.1d
    c. IEEE 802.1stp
    d. IEEE 803.2

16. Which of the following best describes the full-duplex mode?
    a. It uses point-to-point Ethernet connections.
    b. In full-duplex mode collision detection is disabled.
    c. It cannot transmit and receive at the same time.
    d. It can be used on a hub.

17. What does "BASE" stand for in 10BASE-T?
    a. The base length of the network
    b. The amount of data per second
    c. The type of media used
    d. Signaling rate

18. Which Data Link layer devices would you use to connect multiple network
     segments into a single logical network segment? (Select all that apply.)
     a. Bridge
     b. Switch
     c. Router
     d. Gateway

Answers and Explanations

1. **a.** Half-duplex is when one device can send to another device and the other device can do the same, but only one way at a time. This uses a single cable and is similar to a narrow one-way bridge.

2. **d.** The Store and Forward mode has the highest latency because it waits to receive the entire frame, especially a large frame.

3. **a.** Cut Through has the lowest latency of all three modes because it sends the frame as soon as it reads the destination address.

4. **c.** Cut Through reads the first bits in the destination address and the frame is sent before receiving the entire frame. The LAN switch copies only the destination address (the first 6 bytes following the preamble) into its onboard buffers.

5. **b, c.** Cut Through and Fragment Free have fixed latency times because each reads a predetermined portion of the frame before sending out the frame; Cut Through reads 6 bytes and Fragment Free reads 64 bytes.

6. **b.** Because routers limit data to the segment it is intended for and broadcasts are not forwarded, routers create only one broadcast domain and one collision domain per segment.

7. **b.** A full-duplex benefit is that there is 10 Mbps bandwidth in each direction. (The bandwidth could be greater if you are using Fast Ethernet.) So if you have a 10BASE-T network running in full-duplex mode with 8 separate connections to a switch, the bandwidth of each connection is 20 Mbps per connection.

8. **d.** Address learning, forward/filter, and loop avoidance are switch functions, which increase available bandwidth on the network. Address learning keeps track of source addresses and sends the packet directly to the host, so there is no need for a broadcast that can increase traffic and reduce bandwidth. With forward/filter, if the host is on the same segment, the frame is only sent to the host, which reduces traffic. If the loops are removed through the use of STP, the bandwidth is increased because of reduced traffic.

9. **b, c.** Bridges remember the source hardware address of each frame received on an interface and put this information into a MAC database. Bridges can increase the number of collision domains.

10. **a, d.** You can segment the network with bridges and routers, thereby breaking up the collision domains. Bridged networks break up collision domains, but the network is still one large broadcast domain.

11. **a, b, c.** Collisions decrease because some frames are filtered. Total bandwidth is increased because each segment runs at 10 Mbps, not just a single large 10 Mbps segment. Bridges create physically separate network segments to reduce traffic. Traffic stays on the LAN segment if the destination address is on the same LAN. Bridges do not reduce the impact of broadcasts.

12. **a.** Fragment Free waits for 64 bytes to be received before sending out the frame. The 64 bytes extends into the data portion (about 50% of the data) of the frame.

13. **c.** Because routers limit data to the segment it is intended for and broadcasts are not forwarded, routers create only one broadcast domain and one collision domain per segment.

14. **d.** The purpose of the Spanning-Tree Protocol (STP) is to dynamically create a bridged/switched network in which only one path exists between any pair of LAN segments. It was developed to prevent routing loops in a network. The STP will create a loop-free network.

15. **b.** The Spanning-Tree Protocol has frames called Bridge Protocol Data Units (BPDUs), which are sent and received by all switches in the network periodically. The frames aren't forwarded by the switches participating in the spanning tree, but are instead used to set up the spanning-tree topology itself. Catalyst 5000 series switches use IEEE 802.1d to perform this function.

16. **a, b.** Full-duplex uses point-to-point connections and is usually collision-free since it doesn't share bandwidth with any other devices. In order to run full-duplex, you must have the loopback and collision detection disabled.

17. **d.** The "BASE" in 10BASE-T refers to the type of wire signaling rate used.

18. **a, b.** Bridges and switches, which are Data Link layer devices, are used to connect multiple network segments into a single logical network segment. This means that because these devices cannot segment the network like a router can, the network becomes a larger single collision network.

Chapter 3

Virtual LANs

These are the areas that are generally testable on the CCNA examination:

1. Describe Virtual LANs.
2. Describe frame tagging.
3. Describe Inter-Switch Link routing.
4. Describe VLAN Trunk Protocol.

Introduction

Even though Chapter 3 is short, it is now testable in the Version 2 examination. There is a lot of useful information in this chapter, such as what a Virtual LAN is and what it does, as well as a comparison of layer-2 switches and VLANs. (Broadcasts are eliminated and security is improved through VLANs.)

We'll discuss establishing VLAN memberships statically or dynamically. You will learn the pros and cons of each. Then, through the use of frame tagging, you will learn how VLANs receive their identity. The ISL protocol is used to tag information so VLANs can be multiplexed over a trunk link.

Finally, we'll discuss the VTP modes and how the VTP is used to manage all the VLANs in your network.

WHAT IS A VIRTUAL LAN?

A Virtual LAN is a logical grouping of network users. These users are then assigned to administratively defined ports on a switch. VLANs are illustrated in Figure 3-1. *When you create VLANs, you can create smaller broadcast domains within the switch. This is done by assigning different ports in the switch to different subnets. *VLANs act like their own subnet or broadcast domain. This means that broadcast frames are only switched between ports in the same VLAN. What does this really mean? Broadcasts sent out from a node in one VLAN will not be forwarded to a different VLAN. IEEE 802.1P and 802.1Q are standards for VLANs.*

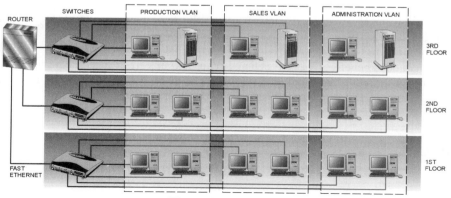

Figure 3-1: VLANs

In a layer-2 (Data Link) switched network, the network is flat. Broadcasts are sent to every device on the network. This causes problems for large networks because if there are too many broadcasts, it will reduce the available bandwidth used to transmit data. Another problem with flat networks is security; all users can see all the devices and can access them on that physical LAN. By creating VLANs, you take care of these problems.

Broadcast Control

To help eliminate broadcasts that usually occur in a layer-2 switched network, VLANs are used in conjunction with layer-3 switches, routers, or route switch modules (RSMs). A VLAN operating on a Catalyst switch limits transmission of unicast, multicast, and broadcast traffic to only the other ports belonging to that VLAN, thereby controlling broadcasts.

Security

The biggest problem with the flat network (layer-2 switches) is security. Layer-2 networks were normally implemented by connecting hubs and switches together with routers. Security was usually done at the router. The problem was that anyone could connect to the physical network and access the network resources on that physical LAN. Also, anyone could use a network analyzer on a hub and see all the traffic in that network. Another problem was that anyone could join a workgroup by just plugging their workstations into the existing hub.

With VLANs and multiple broadcast groups, administrators have control over each port and ultimately each user. Users cannot just plug their workstations into any switch port and have access to network resources.

Another added benefit of VLANs is that, because groups are created according to the network resources a user requires, switches can be configured to inform network management of any unauthorized access to network resources.

Flexibility

Layer-2 switches can only filter a packet based on the MAC address. They do not have the capability to use IP addressing. This can cause a switch to forward all broadcasts.

But because you can assign switch ports to VLAN groups, this gives you the flexibility to add only those users you wish to have in the broadcast domain. The user's physical location doesn't matter in VLANs. *In fact a logical broadcast domain can span multiple physical LAN segments. With a VLAN, your network can be segmented by functions, project team, or applications. VLANs also give you the flexibility to create multiple broadcast domains within a switched network.* Doing this can also help eliminate broadcast storms sometimes caused by faulty network interface cards.

If a VLAN gets too big and you notice that the bandwidth is not sufficient for its needs, you can just create more VLANs to keep the broadcasts from consuming too much bandwidth. The fewer users in a VLAN, the better. More users in the VLAN could be affected by the increased number of broadcasts. *VLANs must be connected to a layer-3 device to be able to talk to each other.*

EXAM TIP: You need to know that VLANs give you the capability to increase the number of collision and broadcast domains in your network. Also, VLANs must be connected to a layer-3 device in order to communicate.

VLAN Memberships

VLANs can be manually set up by the administrator or can be set up dynamically.

- **Dynamic VLANs:** Dynamic VLANs determine a port's VLAN assignment automatically. *The Management Policy Server is used to establish a database of MAC addresses. This can then be used for dynamic addressing of VLANs.*

- **Static VLANs:** Static VLANs are the normal way of creating VLANs, and are the most secure. An administrator must manually change port assignments.

EXAM TIP: There are two types of VLAN memberships: static and dynamic. Know that you can use the Management Policy Server to aid in creating a dynamic VLAN.

Virtual LANs

Identification of VLANs

VLANs can usually span across multiple connected switches. *Because of this, the switches in the switch fabric need to keep track of all the frames and where these frames need to go. Frame tagging is used to keep track of all this information. There are two different types of links in a switched environment:*

- **Access links:** Links can belong to one VLAN only. This is called the native VLAN of the port. *Access link devices (native VLAN) must route their packets through a router in order to communicate with devices outside their VLAN.*

- **Trunk links:** Trunks usually support multiple VLANs. Trunk links can even be used to connect switches to other switches, routers, and servers. *Trunked links can only be used on Fast or Gigabit Ethernets. Trunk links can fall back to their native VLAN if the trunk link fails.*

EXAM TIP: VLANs are important on the exam. Know how VLANs are identified, and that access link devices need a router to communicate outside their VLAN. Trunked links can only be used on Fast or Gigabit Ethernet.

- **Inter-Switch Link (ISL) Protocol:** ISL is used to tag VLAN information onto an Ethernet frame. *Tagging this information allows VLANs to be multiplexed over a trunk link.* By using ISL, you can connect many switches together and at the same time maintain VLAN information as traffic travels between switches on trunk links. *ISL can be used on a switch port and a router interface.* ISL can be used on a Fast Ethernet using half- or full-duplex. ISL has a low-latency, full wire-speed performance. ISL is proprietary to Cisco devices. ISL uses external tagging that will not alter the original frame. When ISL is used, network users do not need to go through a layer-3 device to access a shared server.

  NOTE: In order for ISL to operate properly, each device must be ISL-compatible.

  - The port that a frame is forwarded out of determines if the ISL VLAN information is added to the frame. ISL is added only if the frame goes out through a port configured as a trunk link. If the frame is forwarded out of an access link, the ISL encapsulation is removed from the frame.

- **Frame tagging:** A switch needs to keep track of users and frames in VLANs. Cisco created frame tagging for when a frame travels a trunked link. In frame tagging a frame is given a unique identification that helps to identify which VLAN the frame belongs to. This ID is called the VLAN ID, or color.

EXAM TIP: You need to know that the ISL protocol allows VLANs to be multiplexed over a trunk link. You also need to know that ISL can be used on a switch port or a router interface.

Trunks

Trunk links are 100 or 1000 Mbps point-to-point links between two switches, or between a switch and another switch, router, or server. It is not possible to have trunked links on 10 Mbps links. Trunking gives you the ability to designate a single port as part of multiple VLANs. The greatest positive aspect of trunking is that a server can support two broadcast domains at the same time and a router is not needed between them. *Cisco switches use the Dynamic Trunking Protocol (DTP) to manage trunk negotiation in the Catalyst-switch engine software release 4.2 or later.*

VLAN TRUNK PROTOCOL

VLAN Trunk Protocol (VTP) is used to manage all the VLANs in your network and to provide consistency to the network. With VTP an administrator can add, delete, and rename VLANs. This information is then propagated to all switches.

You must create a VTP server to allow VTP to manage your VLANs in the network. Servers that share VLAN information must have the same domain name. A switch can be a member of only one domain at a time.

VTP Modes

There are three different modes of operation within a VTP domain:

- **Server:** Used on all Catalyst switches. You must have no less than one server in your VTP domain to allow propagation of VLAN information to all parts of the domain. In order to create, add, or delete VLANs in a VTP domain, the switch must be in server mode. If you want to change the VTP information, you must also be in server mode. If a change is made to a switch in server mode, it is then advertised to the whole VTP domain.

- **Client:** Gets its information from VTP servers and can send and receive updates, but cannot make changes. Changes on a client switch cannot be updated to a new VLAN before the VTP server notifies the client switch of the new VLAN. Before a normal switch can become a server, it must first become a client so that it receives all the correct VLAN information.

- **Transparent:** Does not participate in the VTP domain, but will still forward VTP advertisements. VTP transparent switches can add and delete VLANs because a transparent switch keeps its own database and does not share it with other switches.

> **EXAM TIP: DTP is used to manage trunk negotiation in the Catalyst-switch engine software release 4.2 or later. VTP manages all the VLANs in the network and provides consistency to the network. A VTP server is used to manage VLANs. There are three VTP modes: server, client, and transparent. Know what each mode is capable of doing.**

Benefits of VLANs are:

- They simplify moves, adds, and changes
- They reduce administrative costs
- Better control of broadcasts
- They tighten network security
- Distributed traffic load
- Relocation of server into secured locations

1. Which of the following is a VLAN benefit? (Select all that apply.)
   a. It can increase the number of broadcast domains.
   b. It will decrease the number of broadcast domains.
   c. It can increase the number of collision domains.
   d. It will decrease the number of collision domains.

2. Which of the following describes a VLAN? (Select all that apply.)
   a. A logical broadcast domain that can span multiple physical LAN segments.
   b. It can be segmented by functions, project teams, or applications.
   c. It can enable switches to create multiple broadcast domains within a switched network.
   d. VLAN members cannot become members of another VLAN.

3. Which of the following is true about ISL tagging? (Select all that apply.)
   a. SL cannot be enabled on a router.
   b. ISL will change the original frame.
   c. A Cisco proprietary is used to interconnect multiple switches and to maintain VLAN information as traffic goes between switches.
   d. Each device must be ISL-compatible.

4. What modes does VTP operate at? (Select all that apply.)
   a. Native
   b. Server
   c. Client
   d. Transparent

5. After a VLAN is created, which of the following is possible? (Select all that apply.)
   a. It can create smaller broadcast domains within the switch.
   b. It acts like its own subnet or broadcast domain.
   c. Broadcast frames are transmitted to all VLANs.
   d. Broadcast frames are not transmitted to all VLANs.

6. To which of the following must VLANs be connected in order to talk to each other?
   a. Another switch
   b. A hub
   c. A router
   d. A gateway

7. How can VLANs be established? (Select all that apply.)
   a. Statically
   b. Dynamically
   c. A only
   d. None of the above

8. Identify the statements about trunked links that are true. (Select two.)
   a. Trunked links can be used only on Fast or Gigabit Ethernets.
   b. Trunk links can fall back to their native VLAN if the trunk link fails.
   c. Trunked links can be used on 10BASE-T Ethernets.
   d. If the trunk fails it cannot fall back to its native VLAN.

9. Cisco switches use which of the following to manage trunk negotiation in the Catalyst-switch engine software release 4.2 or later?
   a. ISL
   b. VTP
   c. STP
   d. DTP

10. How can a normal switch become a server?
    a. It must first become a VTP client.
    b. Promote it directly to a VTP server.
    c. A normal switch cannot become a server.
    d. None of the above

Answers and Explanations

1. **a, c.** VLANs give you the capability to increase the number of broadcast and collision domains in your network.

2. **a, b, c.** In fact, a logical broadcast domain can span multiple physical LAN segments. With a VLAN, your network can be segmented by functions, project team, or applications. VLANs also give you the flexibility to create multiple broadcast domains within a switched network.

3. **c, d.** ISL is proprietary to Cisco devices. You can connect many switches together and at the same time maintain VLAN information as traffic travels between switches on trunk links. In order for ISL to operate properly, each device must be ISL-compatible.

4. **b, c, d.** There are three different modes of operation within a VTP domain: server, client, and transparent modes.

5. **a, b, d.** When you create VLANs, you can create smaller broadcast domains within the switch. VLANs act like their own subnet or broadcast domain. This means that broadcast frames are only switched between ports in the same VLAN. Broadcasts sent out from a node in one VLAN will not be forwarded to a different VLAN.

6. **c.** Access link devices (native VLAN) must route their packets through a router in order to communicate with devices outside their VLAN.

7. **a, b.** VLANs can be manually set up by the administrator or can be set up dynamically. They are called static VLANs and dynamic VLANs. There are two types of VLAN memberships: static and dynamic.

8. **a, b.** Trunked links can be used only on Fast or Gigabit Ethernets. Trunk links can fall back to their native VLAN if the trunk link fails.

9. **d.** Cisco switches use the Dynamic Trunking Protocol (DTP) to manage trunk negotiation in the Catalyst-switch engine software release 4.2 or later.

10. **a.** Before a normal switch can become a server, it must first become a client so that it receives all the correct VLAN information.

Chapter

Router Configuration and the IOS

These are the areas that are generally testable on the CCNA examination:

1. Use the setup feature on a Cisco router.

2. Log into a router in both User and Privileged modes.

3. Find commands using the help facilities.

4. Use commands on a router using the editing commands.

5. Set the router passwords, identification, and banners.

6. Configure and interface with IP addresses and subnet masks.

7. Copy the configuration to NVRAM.

Router Configuration and the IOS

Chapter 4

Introduction

This chapter is full of things that you need to memorize; not only for the exam, but for the real world. We will start with the Setup mode and the command and procedures used to get into this mode. You will learn that the preferred method to configure your router is the Command-Line Interface (CLI).

You must know how to get into User mode and how to get from User to Privileged mode with the enable command. Learn what the prompt looks like as you move from User to Privileged mode. Also, know what the router prompt looks like when you change from Privileged to Global Configuration mode.

We will also look at the help commands and the editing commands.

You must be proficient with saving your router's configuration file and the command to view the configuration. Be aware that there are two configuration files, the running-config and startup-config.

The router has five ways to keep it secure with passwords. I will show you all five ways and how to set the passwords on the router.

Then we'll move on to how to add a message-of-the-day banner. Finally, the most important configuration on the router is applying an IP address to the router's interface and turning on the interface.

CISCO ROUTER IOS

The Cisco Internetworking Operating System (IOS) was created to deliver network services and enable networked applications. The Cisco IOS runs on most Cisco routers and on some Cisco switches.

Bringing Up a Router

When you first bring up a Cisco router, it will run a power-on self test (POST) and then look for and load the Cisco IOS from flash memory. The IOS loads and then looks for a valid configuration file called "startup-config", which is stored by default in nonvolatile RAM (NVRAM).

Note: The reload command will reload the startup configuration into memory.

The router will put you in Setup mode if there is no configuration in NVRAM. This is a step-by-step process to help you configure a router. ***You can also enter Setup mode at any time from the command line by typing the command SETUP from Global Configuration mode.***

As you move through Setup mode, you will see entries in brackets like these: [ ]. The default answers for the questions asked in Setup mode are located in these brackets. To accept the default answer just press the ENTER key.

Setup Mode

You actually have two options when using Setup mode: Basic Management and Extended Setup. Basic Management only gives you enough configurations to allow connectivity to the router, while Extended Setup allows you to configure some global parameters as well as interface configuration parameters.

Command-Line Interface

The best way to configure a router is with the Command-Line Interface (CLI) because it gives you the most flexibility. To use the CLI, just say no to "entering the Initial Configuration Dialog" when the router is first turned on.

Logging into the Router

When you first turn on the router some interface status messages appear. At this time press ENTER and the "Router>" prompt will appear. Later, if you add a password to the User Exec mode, you will press ENTER and use a password if necessary; otherwise you will just press ENTER. At this point you are in User mode, which is mainly used to view statistics, and can be used to log into Privileged mode. Privileged mode is the only way to view and change the configuration of a Cisco router. ***Privileged mode is entered by using the enable command. The enable command is:***

    Router>**enable**
    Router#

NOTE: To make it real simple to log into Privileged mode, type **enable** and press the ENTER key.

Notice the ">" after Router. This means you are in the User mode. "Router#" indicates you are in Privileged mode. You can go back to User mode by using the **disable** command:

> Router#**disable**
> Router>

You can also type **exit** from the Privileged mode prompt to log out. If you are in Global Configuration mode (that's where you are after you type **config t**), type **exit** and you will be returned to Privileged mode.

> Router#**exit**
> Router>

EXAM TIP: You can also enter Setup mode at any time from the command line by typing the command SETUP from the Global Configuration mode. Privileged mode is entered by using the enable command. You can go back to User mode by using the disable command. You also need to know what the router prompt looks like in each mode.

Two Command Exec Modes

The two Command Exec modes are: USER EXEC mode (User mode) and ENABLE mode (Privileged mode). Sometimes the Command Exec mode is called Cisco's command interpreter. Figure 4-1 illustrates how User mode is used to access Privileged mode.

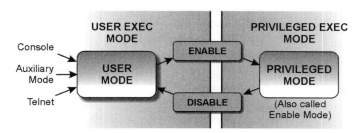

Figure 4-1: Accessing Privileged Mode

- **User mode:** Is used for common tasks like checking the router's status and viewing basic system information. But in this mode, your capabilities are very limited.

- **Privileged mode:** Also called "Enabled mode" because of the command used to enter the mode. Only privileged commands can be executed there. This is where you can change the configuration of the router.

NOTE: When you first log in to a router you see a User Exec mode prompt. ***You can type "?" to get a list of commands at any time.*** If you are typing a command and receive "%INCOMPLETE COMMAND", what can you do? Well, retype the command followed by a "?". Type "Logout" at any time to log off the router. The router will time-out and log you out automatically after a period of inactivity.

Overview of Router Modes

To configure from the CLI, type *config* while in Privileged mode. This puts you in Global Configuration mode. While in this mode you can make changes to the running-config. When you make changes in this mode they can affect the whole router, hence the term Global Configuration mode.

The running-config is the current configuration running on the router, and it is stored in Dynamic RAM (DRAM). (RAM also provides for packet caching and buffering.) To change the running-config you must use the config terminal command. There is another configuration file on the router called startup-config. To change the configuration file stored in NVRAM, use the config memory command. To change a router configuration stored on a TFTP host, use the config network command. We will get into how to apply the various configuration commands later in this chapter.

CLI Prompts

It is important to understand the different prompts as you work your way through the different levels. Always check your prompts before making any changes to a router's configuration. For example, if you are in Global Configuration mode and make a change, it will affect the entire router configuration.

EXAM TIP: On the exam you may receive questions that require you to know which command prompt is associated with each mode level. Review the following information and learn to recognize the different levels.

```
Router>                              User mode
Router>enable
Router#                              Privileged mode
Router#Config t
Router(config)#                      Global config mode
Router(config)#interface e0
Router(config-if)#                   Interface config mode
```

NOTE: Basically, look at what follows the word "Router".

Help Commands

You can use the Cisco advanced editing features to help you configure your router. Entering a question mark (?) at any prompt displays a list of commands available from that prompt.

NOTE: If you place a space between the command and the ?, the response you get will be different, as shown in Table 4-1.

Table 4-1: Help Commands

Type	You Get	
?	Help for all commands.	
Help	Gives text of help commands.	
Com?	List of commands that start with "COM".	
Command ?	List help on all "command" options.	
COM<TAB>more than one	Will spell out command or do nothing if there is more than one option. The TAB is used to complete commands.	

Editing Commands

Key commands to retrieve from the command history buffer are shown in Table 4-2:

Table 4-2: Editing Commands

Type	You Get
Up-arrow or CTRL+P	Most recently used command. ("P" means previous.)
Down-arrow or CTRL+N	Displays next command.
CTRL+A	Moves the cursor to the first character of the command.
CTRL+E	Moves the cursor directly to the end of the command.
ESC+B	Moves backward one word.
ESC+F	Moves forward one word.

NOTE: You can turn off the IOS Editing feature with the **terminal no editing** command.
To review the command history buffer, use the show history command.

EXAM TIP: Memorize both of the above charts. It is very likely that you will see some of this information on the exam.

These are the areas that are generally testable on the CCNA examination:

Configuration process and the configuration file:

• Manage configuration files from Privileged Exec mode.

• Control router passwords, identification, and banner.

• Enter an initial configuration using the setup command.

• Copy and manipulate configuration files.

• Prepare the initial configuration of your router and enable IP.

VIEWING AND SAVING CONFIGURATIONS

As you are going through the setup options in Setup mode, you will be asked if you want to use the configuration you created. If you say yes, it will copy the configuration running in DRAM, known as running-config, to NVRAM and name the file startup-config. From that point on, every time the router is rebooted, the startup-config is used.

Manage Configuration Files in Privileged Mode

The router's configuration information is contained in configuration files. As previously mentioned, there are two basic configurations for each router: startup and running. The startup configuration is kept in NVRAM and is accessed when the router is first started, then copied and placed into DRAM. To see the router's startup configuration, type **show startup-config** (or show configuration). Running configuration is the configuration from NVRAM placed in DRAM at startup. When you are in Global Configuration mode, which is accessed by typing **config t**, any changes you make will change the running-config. After you make any changes to the running-config, make sure you copy it to the startup-config by typing **copy running-config startup-config**. You will learn more on this in the next chapter.

Figure 4-2 illustrates managing configuration files in Privileged mode.

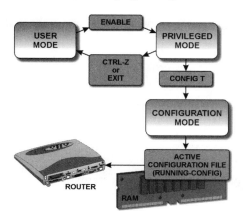

Figure 4-2: Managing Configuration Files in Privileged Mode

Passwords

Five different passwords can be used to secure your router: enable secret, enable password, virtual terminal password, auxiliary password, and console password. The first two passwords are used to set your enable password, which is used to secure Privileged mode. The other three are used to configure a password when User mode is accessed.

Enable Secret

Enable secret is a one-way password used in versions 10.3 and up. It has precedence over the enable password when it exists. Sometimes the enable secret password is called the encrypted secret password.

> Router#**Config t**
> Router(Config)#**Enable secret XXXX** (where XXXX is the password)

CTRL+Z will take you back to Privileged mode, allowing you to back up the config file.

Enable Password

Enable password is used when there is no enable secret and when using older software.

> Router#**Config t**
> Router(Config)#**Enable password XXXX**

NOTE: If the router is not configured with an enable secret password, the enable password would be used.

Virtual Terminal Password

Virtual terminal password is used for Telnet sessions into the router. You can change the vty password at any time, but it must first be specified or you won't be able to telnet into the router. You can specify the vty password during the setup mode or by typing:

Router#**Config t**
Router(Config)#**Line vty 0 4**
    Login
    Password XXXX
Router(Config)#**CTRL+Z**

NOTE: vty 0 4 specifies the number of Telnet sessions allowed in the router. The **login** command actually tells the router to display a prompt. Routers that are not running the Enterprise edition of the Cisco IOS default to five VTY lines, 0-4. However, if you use the Enterprise edition, you will have many more lines.

Auxiliary Password

Auxiliary password is used to set a password for the auxiliary port. This port is used to connect a modem to a router for remote console connections.

Router#**Config t**
Router(Config)#**Line aux 0**
    Login
    Password XXXX
Router(Config)#**CTRL+Z**

NOTE: The command line "Line aux 0" indicates that the auxiliary port will be configured with a password.

Console Password

Console password is used to set the console port password. It can be set up manually only by typing:

Router#**Config t**
Router(Config)#**Line con 0**
    Login
    Password XXXX
Router(Config)#**CTRL+Z**

NOTE: The command line "Line con 0" indicates that the console port will be configured with a password.

Service Password-Encryption

Service Password-Encryption is a global command that encrypts passwords in the config file so they are not seen in clear text.

EXAM TIP: All you need to know in this section is how to set the five different passwords. Be aware that passwords are case-sensitive. For example, if CISCO is your password, typing Cisco will not grant you access to the router.

Entering a Banner

Placing a banner on your router will allow that banner to be displayed whenever anyone logs into your Cisco router.

MOTD

The *MOTD* command is **banner motd** #. Motd stands for "message of the day". You must start a motd banner with a delimiting character of your choice. Notice that banners start with a delimiting character like "#".

EXAM TIP: You just might see the "banner motd #" command in the near future. Cisco commands must be typed correctly or they will not work. For example, typing "motd banner #" will not work.

Exec Banner

With Exec banner you can configure a line-activation banner to be displayed when an incoming connection to a VTY line is created.

Incoming Banner

Incoming banner is displayed on terminals connected to reverse Telnet lines.

Login Banner

Login banner is displayed on all connected terminals. This banner is displayed after the MOTD, but before the login prompts. To globally disable the login banner, you must delete the login banner with the "no banner login" command.

ROUTER INTERFACES

Router Interfaces is one of the most important configurations of the router. If you don't configure the interfaces, the router will not function. A router interface is the interface used to connect to a network segment.

Bring Up an Interface

You can turn an interface off with the interface command **shutdown** or turn it on with the **no shutdown** command. By default all interfaces are shut down. This means that when the router is first turned on, no interfaces are activated, and the router will not route data until the interfaces are turned on.

Configuring an IP Address on an Interface

To configure IP addresses on an interface, use the IP address command from Interface Configuration mode. But to really activate the interface you have to use the **no shutdown** command, as seen below.

Router(config)#**int e0**
Router(config-if)#**ip address 170.14.10.5 255.255.0.0**
Router(config-if)#**no shut**

Remember that some Cisco commands can be abbreviated. An example of configuring an Ethernet 0 interface is shown below. Notice the three different ways to see the same command.

- interface ethernet 0
- interface e0
- int e0

NOTE: The **no shut** command turns on the interface. *Use the show interface e0* command to see if it is administratively shut down, which means that someone used the shutdown command on that interface. **Show running-config** will also show you if the interface is shut down. *You can also use show running-config to view IP addresses for the router's interfaces, including secondary addresses.*

You must use the secondary command if you want to add a second subnet address to an interface. If you just type another IP address without the secondary command and press ENTER, the existing IP address and mask for that interface will be replaced.

Router(config)#**int e0**
Router(config-if)#**ip address 172.16.20.2 255.255.0.0 secondary**
Router(config-if)**CTRL+Z**

Chapter 4

Testing with the Show Interface Command

The Show Interface command is **show interface s0**. This command allows you to view the following:

- *If the interface is up and the line protocol is up, the interface is up and running.* "interface" refers to the Physical layer, which is "up" when it receives a carrier detect. "Line protocol" refers to the Data Link layer, which relies on keep-alives from the connecting end.

- *If the interface is up but the line protocol is down*, there is either a problem with the connection clocking (keep-alives) or possibly a framing issue. Check the keep-alives on both ends to make sure they match. Make sure the clock rate is set. Additionally, make sure the encapsulation type is the same on both ends.

- *If the interface is down and so is the line protocol*, it means there's an interface or cable problem; a hardware problem.

- *If the interface is administratively down and the line protocol is also down, then the interface is disabled or the shutdown command was used.* Use the no shutdown command in the interface configuration.

> **EXAM TIP:** Study these entries. You may get a question that will give you a symptom and you have to explain the cause, or you may get the opposite type question.

Hostname

You can change the name your router displays by using the *hostname command.*

```
Router#config t
Router(config)#hostname RouterC   (RouterC is the name of the router)
RouterC(config-line)#CTRL+Z
```

You can change the clock rate on a DCE router with the #clock rate 56000 command. Notice the space between clock and rate.

Using the Show Controllers Command

Use the **show controllers** command to view information about the physical interface. This command also gives you the type of serial cable plugged into a serial port. This will usually be a DTE cable, which plugs into a Data Service Unit (DSU).

NOTE: This is the only command with a space after the command serial. The "s" below represents serial.

> Router#**sh controllers s 0**

IOS COMMANDS

Cisco routers have their own operating system, the Cisco IOS. You must know its commands for the test.

The most common Cisco IOS command is "show", as shown in Table 4-3. IOS can understand abbreviations of commands, such as show, sho, or sh. This is true of most of the IOS commands. On version 10.3 and earlier, however, you have to write the full command. Additional Cisco IOS commands are listed in Table 4-4.

Table 4-3: Cisco IOS Show Commands

Command	Result
Show Version	Displays the current version of the Cisco IOS, how long the router has been up, how the system started, where the system was loaded from, the interfaces the POST found, and the configuration register.
Show Memory	Shows how the management system allocated memory for different purposes.
Show Processes	Displays the active processes on your router.
Show Stacks	Monitors the stack use of processes and interrupt routines, and, if the last reboot was caused by a crash, displays the reason for the crash.
Show Buffers	Displays statistics for router buffer pools; shows the size of the Small, Middle, Big, Very Big, Large, and Huge Buffers.
Show Flash	Describes the flash memory and displays the size of files and the amount of free flash memory.
Show Running-Config	Details the running configuration file.
Show Startup-Config	Displays the configuration stored in NVRAM.
Show Interfaces	Displays the status of all the hardware interfaces installed on the router.
Show Protocols	Displays which protocols are configured on the router.
Show IP Protocol	Shows the protocol in more detail.
Show History	Shows your history of commands.

Table 4-4: Cisco IOS Commands

Command	Result
enable	Enters Privileged mode.
enable password newpassword	Sets/changes the Privileged mode password.
banner motd #	Set/change banner.
setup	Will start the automatic setup; the same as when you first boot the router.
copy flash tftp	Copies Flash to TFTP server.
copy tftp flash	Restores Flash from TFTP server.
copy run tftp	Copies the current running-config to the TFTP server.
copy tftp run	Restores the current running-config from the TFTP server.
sh ip route	Displays the route of the IP.
sh access-list	This command is followed by the number of an access list; displays that access list.

Review Questions

1. How do you log onto Exec mode?
    a. Type enable and press ENTER.
    b. Press ENTER and the password, if necessary.
    c. Type disable and press ENTER.
    d. Type quit or exit and press ENTER.

2. To disable the IOS editing feature type:
    a. no terminal editing
    b. quit terminal editing
    c. terminal no editing
    d. disable editing

3.   Which of the following editing commands is used to move to the beginning of the command line?
      a. CTRL+A
      b. CTRL+B
      c. ALT+A
      d. CTRL+P

4.   Which of the following editing commands is used to move to the end of the command line?
      a. CTRL+B
      b. ALT+B
      c. ALT+E
      d. CTRL+E

5.   Which of the following editing commands is used to move backward one word?
      a. CTRL+B
      b. ESC+B
      c. TAB+B
      d. ALT+B

6.   Which of the following editing commands is used to move forward one word?
      a. CTRL+F
      b. SHIFT+F
      c. ESC+F
      d. ALT+F

7.   Which of the following editing commands is used to repeat the previous command entry?
      a. SHIFT+P
      b. CTRL+P
      c. TAB+P
      d. ALT+P

8. Which of the following editing commands is used to show the command history buffer?
   a. no editing
   b. disable editing
   c. show history
   d. show editing

9. Which of the following editing commands is used to complete an entry?
   a. TAB
   b. SHIFT+TAB
   c. ALT+TAB
   d. CTRL+TAB

10. How do you change the password on a console?
    a. line aux 0
    b. line con 0
    c. line vty 0 4
    d. login con 0

11. Which of the following are types of passwords used in securing Cisco routers? (Select all that apply.)
    a. Enable secret
    b. Enable password
    c. Virtual terminal password
    d. Auxiliary password
    e. Console password

12. Which of the following passwords would you use when there is no enable secret password?
    a. Virtual terminal password
    b. Console password
    c. Auxiliary password
    d. Enable password

13. Which of the following passwords is used on versions 10.3 and up to replace enable password?
    a. Enable secret
    b. Console password
    c. Virtual terminal password
    d. Auxiliary password

14. Which command would set the encrypted secret password to cisco?
    a. password cisco
    b. enable secret cisco
    c. enable secret CISCO
    d. secret password cisco

15. Which command would you use to add a banner whenever anyone logs on to a Cisco router?
    a. # motd banner
    b. banner motd #
    c. banner # motd #
    d. motd banner #

16. Which of the following is a true statement about banners?
    a. Banners are mandatory on a router.
    b. Banners must start with a #.
    c. Banners need to start with a delimiting character.
    d. Banners must end with a #.

17. How do you change the clock rate on a DCE router?
    a. #clock rate 56000
    b. >clock rate 56000
    c. #clockrate 56000
    d. #clock rate 56K

18. What specific commands can you use to configure interface Ethernet 0? (Select three.)
    a. interface e0
    b. e0 interface
    c. int e0
    d. e0 int
    e. interface ethernet 0
    f. ethernet 0 interface

19. What command do you use to change the name of your router to Florida?
    a. Host name Florida
    b. Hostname Florida
    c. Name Change Florida
    d. Florida Hostname

20. After you have delete the startup configuration in the NVRAM, what mode would you be in when you start the router again?
    a. Setup mode
    b. NVRAM mode
    c. No mode; you don't have startup-config.
    d. User mode

21. What command do you use to display the command history buffer for routers?
    a. Router>show history buffer
    b. Router>show history
    c. Router>sh command history buffer
    d. Router>sh cmd buffer

22. If you are in Global Configuration mode, which of the following commands takes you out of Global mode and puts you back into Privileged mode?
    a. CTRL+Z
    b. End
    c. Done
    d. Exit

23. What do the brackets [ ] in the Setup mode mean?
    a. Default answers for the questions
    b. Nothing, they are parentheses ( ).
    c. Prompts to answer the question
    d. Change all the default parameters.

Answers and Explanations

1. **b.** If you add a password to the User Exec mode, you will press ENTER and use a password if necessary; otherwise you will just press ENTER.

2. **c.** You can turn off the IOS Editing feature with the terminal no editing command.

3. **a.** CTRL+A moves the cursor to the first character of the command.

4. **d.** CTRL+E moves the cursor directly to the end of the command.

5. **b.** ESC+B moves backward one word.

6. **c.** ESC+F moves forward one word.

7. **b.** CTRL+P or the up-arrow will display the most recently used command. ("P" means previous.)

8. **c.** To review the command history buffer, use the show history command. The show history command shows the history of commands.

9. **a.** The TAB is used to complete commands.

10. **b.** The command line "Line con 0" indicates that the console port will be configured with a password.

11. **a, b, c, d, e.** Five different passwords can be used to secure your router: enable secret, enable password, virtual terminal password, auxiliary password, and console password. The first two passwords are used to set your enable password, which is used to secure Privileged mode. The other three are used to configure a password when User mode is accessed.

12. **d.** If the router is not configured with an enable secret password, the enable password would be used.

13. **a.** Enable secret is a one-way password used in versions 10.3 and up. It has precedence over the enable password when it exists.

14. **b.** The command is Enable secret XXXX (where XXXX is the password). Sometimes the enable secret password is called the encrypted secret password.

15. **b.** The MOTD command is "banner motd #". Motd stands for "message of the day". You must start a motd banner with a delimiting character of your choice. Notice that banners start with a delimiting character like "#". Cisco commands must be typed correctly or they will not work.

16. **c.** You must start a motd banner with a delimiting character of your choice.

17. **a.** You can change the clock rate on a DCE router with the #clock rate 56000 command. Notice the space between clock and rate.

18. **a, c, e.** Some Cisco commands can be abbreviated. Three different ways to configure an "Ethernet 0 interface" are: interface ethernet 0, interface e0, and int e0.

19. **b.** You can change the name your router displays by using the hostname command Hostname XXXX (where XXXX is the new router name).

20. **a.** The router will put you in Setup mode if there is no configuration in NVRAM. This is a step-by-step process to help you configure a router.

21. **b.** To review the command history buffer, use the show history command.

22. **d.** If you are in Global Configuration mode (that's where you are after you type config t), type exit, and you will be returned to Privileged mode.

23. **a.** As you move through Setup mode, you will see entries in brackets like these [ ]. The default answers for the questions asked in Setup mode are located in these brackets. To accept the default answer just press the ENTER key.

Chapter

5

Managing a Cisco Router

Objectives

These are the areas that are generally testable on the CCNA examination:

1. Examine router elements (RAM, ROM, CDP, SHOW).

2. Back up a Cisco IOS to a TFTP server.

3. Upgrade or restore a Cisco IOS from a TFTP server.

4. Back up and restore a Cisco router configuration using a TFTP server.

5. Use the Cisco Discover Protocol to gather information about neighbor devices.

6. Create a host table on a router and resolve hostnames to IP addresses.

7. Verify your IP host table.

8. Use the OSI model to test IP.

Introduction

This is probably the only area that you may want to get your hands on an actual router and practice the commands, but it isn't necessary.

In this chapter we will discuss the four types of memory located in the router, what is located in each type, and their attributes. Flash is the default location of the IOS. NVRAM stores the startup configuration file, and is also where the configuration register is located. RAM is used to store the running configuration and routing tables, and for caching and packet buffers.

Next, you will learn what happens when the router boots up.

Upgrading/backing up an IOS image is an important aspect of your router to maintain. You will learn to use the **copy tftp flash** command to upgrade an IOS image. Conversely, the **copy flash tftp** can be used to store your current IOS if the IOS in flash becomes corrupt. This is called backing up your router's IOS.

To change the location of the IOS the system uses at bootup, you will use the boot system command. The router will try to load from flash, then from the TFTP server, and finally ROM.

You must know that the **copy run start** command will copy the running-config to the startup-config, and the purpose for this. You will also learn that the **copy start run** command will copy the startup-config to the running-config. Next, the backup command **copy run tftp** will place a backup copy of the running-config onto the TFTP server. Also, you will learn about using the **show running-config** and **show startup-config** commands to view each of these files.

Finally, you will learn the features of CDP. I'll show you how to build host tables and use the Telnet features.

PORT OR CONNECTION TYPES

Most Cisco routers have a console and an auxiliary port. All Cisco routers have a console port for local access, usually from a computer using a terminal emulator. The auxiliary port is used for dial-in access, also from a terminal emulator. This port allows you to connect a modem to the router, which can then be dialed into and configured. The ports of a Cisco router are shown in Figure 5-1.

Figure 5-1: Cisco Router Ports

TYPES OF MEMORY ON A ROUTER

RAM

When the router is turned on, RAM (often called DRAM or Dynamic Random Access Memory) is used for storage of data and programs. *It also stores the running configuration and routing tables. Finally, it is used for caching and packet buffers.*

> **EXAM TIP:** It is important for you to know that RAM is used to store the running configuration and routing tables, and for caching and packet buffers. Usually, you only need to know that the running configuration is stored here.

ROM

ROM (Read-Only Memory) is used to store a bootable IOS image, but not the one used for normal operation. Instead, consider this a backup copy. ROM contains code used to boot the router until the router knows where to get the full IOS image. POST is also located here. *The four areas of ROM microcode are: bootstrap code, POST code, ROM monitor, and partial IOS.*

> **EXAM TIP:** Just memorize these four parts of the ROM microcode.

Flash Memory

Flash memory is usually found in EEPROM (Electronic Erasable Programmable Read Only Memory) or a PCMCIA card, and is used to store the full IOS image. *Flash memory is also the default location of the IOS.* This is where the router gets its

IOS at boot time. Flash is an erasable, reprogrammable ROM that holds the operating system image. Flash memory gives you the option to "flash" the router and perform upgrades without removing and replacing chips on the motherboard. The information located in Flash is retained even when the router is turned off.

NVRAM

NVRAM means nonvolatile RAM. *It stores the initial or startup configuration file.* Because NVRAM is nonvolatile, it retains its information even when the router is rebooted or shut down. *NVRAM also stores the configuration register.*

Configuration Register

The configuration register is a 16-bit register used to control how the router boots up and where to locate the IOS image. It also knows how to use the startup configuration stored in NVRAM.

> **EXAM TIP: You must know that the Flash is the default location of the IOS. NVRAM stores the startup configuration file, and is where the configuration register is located.**

NOTE: All of the above types of memory are permanent except for RAM. Additionally, Cisco routers do not have hard disks.

PHYSICAL INTERFACES

The IOS commands call them interfaces, but they are really just plugs or ports. The physical interfaces are usually located either on the rear of the router (attached to the motherboard) or as a separate module.

THE ROUTER STARTUP PROCEDURE

When the router first powers up, it performs a POST (power-on self test) that does a routine check of the router's hardware. The POST then checks the CPU, memory, and all interfaces to make sure they are operational. Table 5-1 shows what happens when the POST is complete.

Table 5-1: POST

*Type of Memory	What's In It	What It Does
ROM	Bootstrap	Loads bootstrap
Flash (default) TFTP ROM	Cisco IOS	Locates and loads operating system (the IOS)
NVRAM	Configuration file or enters Setup mode	Locates and loads config file

NOTE: The TFTP is not a type of memory, but a secondary location of the Cisco IOS. We'll discuss the TFTP later. There are three ways or sources to configure a IOS on a Cisco device: by the config t command (Terminal), NVRAM, or on the TFTP server.

EXAM TIP: Memorize this chart. You must know what is located in each step. These steps are in sequence.

The startup process in more detail is as follows:

- The bootstrap routine is located in ROM, which is on the CPU card. When the bootstrap routine is executed it searches for the default IOS located in Flash. *The router first tries to locate the IOS from Flash. If an IOS cannot be found, ROM checks the TFTP server, then will use the IOS located in the ROM itself.*

- How does ROM know where to find the IOS? There are two ways to configure the location of the IOS you wish to use. The first option is the configuration register (located in ROM). You put in the appropriate value (for example, 0x2102, is the default), and then, when the router boots up, ROM will know which IOS to use. The preferred second option, using the Boot System command, will be explained later in this chapter.

A good thing to remember is that if you have only one IOS in Flash, you can get the filename that is currently running by using the **show flash** command. If there is more than one IOS in Flash, the **show flash** command will list all files in Flash, but will not indicate which one is currently running. If you have more than one Cisco IOS in Flash, you should type **show version**, although I don't know any practical reason for having more than one IOS in Flash because the memory in Flash is extremely limited.

Once the IOS is loaded and operating properly, the operating system then determines the hardware and software components and lists its findings on the console terminal.

Next, ROM searches for a configuration file. The startup configuration file in NVRAM is then loaded into RAM. It is important to understand that the startup-config file is copied to RAM and is then called the running-config.

If there is no valid configuration in NVRAM, the operating system will put you into a *"question-driven initial configuration dialog" referred to as the system Configuration mode. This mode is also called the setup dialog.*

EXAM TIP: All of the information must be learned for the exam.

These are the areas that are generally testable on the CCNA examination:

Managing IOS images:

- Identify the main Cisco IOS commands for the router startup.

- List the commands to load Cisco IOS software from: Flash memory, TFTP server, or ROM.

- Prepare to back up, upgrade, and load a backup Cisco IOS software image.

FLASH MEMORY

Flash, as you already know, is the normal location of the IOS used by the router. Flash memory is writable and used for permanent storage. Flash is the best storage for files that need to be retained in the event that the router loses power.

Upgrading/Backing Up an IOS Image into Flash Memory

Before you can upgrade the IOS you need to copy the new IOS image into the TFTP server's default directory. You can then use the copy command from the router to copy the file into Flash memory. The command is *copy tftp flash. Copy is the command or action to take, tftp is where the IOS is copied from, and flash is the destination.* After you have completed copying from a TFTP server to flash and are in the process of examining the contents of Flash, you see several exclamation points (!). The exclamation points indicate that one UDP segment has been transferred.

* NOTE: Cisco IOS does not support FTP. It only supports TFTP that is UDP-based.

Before you perform the backup of IOS, use the "ping" command to ensure that you have connectivity to the TFTP server. If the ping is successful, use the copy command.

Router#**copy flash tftp** (Notice that you are in Privileged mode to do this.)

NOTE: For **copy flash tftp** to work, the TFTP server must have a default directory specified where a copy of the IOS is located. This is just a shared file to place the copy of the IOS.

EXAM TIP: The "copy tftp flash" command is used to upgrade an IOS image. The "copy flash tftp" command will back up the current IOS in the tftp server. In case the IOS in Flash becomes corrupt, you can use the copy of tftp flash to restore your current IOS from the tftp server back to Flash. This is called backing up your router's IOS.

After you use the **copy tftp flash** command you will be prompted for additional information:

- The IP address or hostname of the TFTP server

- The name of the file

- Whether there is enough space available for this file in Flash memory. If not, you will be asked if you want the router to erase old files to make room for the IOS.

NOTE: Here is what the full command would look like:

(IP address)   (file name)
copy tftp flash 172.5.4.3 c2500-d-l_113-5.bin

Changing the IOS Location to be Used During Bootup

If you do not wish to use the default location (Flash) of the IOS, enter **boot system tftp ios_filename tftp_ip_address**. Remember that boot system is the command, followed by the location you wish to boot the IOS, the IOS file name, and, finally, the IP address of the TFTP server. You can also use the **boot system ROM** command to use the IOS located in ROM. If you want to revert back to the default, use the **boot system flash** command.

Finally, if you need to boot the system from a file on the network called "beta", you would use the following command: **boot network tftp beta (IP address)**.

EXAM TIP: Know exactly what the boot system command will do. The router will try to load from Flash, then from the TFTP server, and finally from ROM.

The boot system command at startup determines from where the IOS is loaded. If you want to permanently delete the IOS, use the *"squeeze" command*.

The most used Cisco IOS commands are:

- Show Version: Displays the current version of the Cisco IOS. *Also displays information about the system hardware (RAM/ROM), software version, names of configuration files, and boot images. It also shows the current configuration register value.*
  Router#**show version**

EXAM TIP: Know what the "show version" command will display.

- Show Processes: Displays the active processes on your router.

  Router#**show processes**

- Show Memory: Displays how the management system has allocated memory for different purposes.

  Router#**show memory**

- Show Stacks: Monitors the stack use of processes and interrupts routing, and if the reboot was the result of a crash, displays the reason for the last system reboot.

  Router#**show stacks**

- Show Flash: Describes Flash memory and reveals both the size of the file and the amount of free Flash memory.

  Router#**show flash**

- Show Interfaces: Shows the hardware interfaces installed on the router, and their status. The show interfaces command will show the status of each interface. The show protocols command will also do this.

  Router#**sh int e0**

- Show Protocols: Details which protocols are configured on the router.

  Router#**show protocols**

- Show IP Protocol: Displays the protocol in more detail.

  RouterC#**show ip protocol**

EXAM TIP: Learn what these commands do.

MANUAL ROUTER CONFIGURATION

To manually configure the router, you must be in Configuration mode, which can be accessed only from within the Privileged mode. Begin by typing the **enable** command in User mode.

    Router>**enable**
    Router#

Enter the Configuration mode by typing **config** and pressing ENTER. You will be given three choices. Normally, you will use config terminal (**config t**) to configure commands from the terminal.

Config memory (**config mem**) executes configuration commands stored in NVRAM, and will copy the startup-config to the running-config.

Config network (**config net**) is used to retrieve router configuration information from a network TFTP server. When using **config net**, you must supply the IP address or hostname of the network TFTP server.

> **EXAM TIP: For this area you normally only need to know that the config t command places you into Global Configuration mode.**

Be careful when you make changes in Configuration mode, because changes are placed into the running configuration file (RAM) every time the return key is pressed at the end of the command line. This means that while in Configuration mode, the changes are acted upon immediately.

Managing Configuration Files

As stated in the last chapter, there are two configuration files on your router: one in NVRAM (startup config) and one in RAM (what the router uses during operation). The router copies the config file from NVRAM into RAM as part of the boot process. Outside the router, config files can be stored as an ASCII text file on a TFTP Server, a floppy disk, a hard drive, or some other location.

The best way of managing your configuration files is to copy them to your TFTP Server, using the **copy running-config tftp** command. Doing this gives you a critically important backup of the router configuration. If your backup is ever needed, you would use the copy tftp running-config command to load the backup configuration file to the current running configuration file. The process as it would appear on a router is shown in the following:

Router>**enable**
RouterC#**copy run tftp**
Remote host ()? **172.6.20.2**
Name of configuration file to write (routerc-confg)?**return**
Write file routerc-confg on host 172.16.20.2 (confirm)**return**

NOTE: By default, -confg is added to the end of the router's hostname to create its filename. For example, Router-confg.

The copy command is used to move config files between RAM, NVRAM, and a TFTP server.

- After you make changes to the running-config, you must use the **copy running-config startup-config** command. This will update the startup configuration file with the current running configuration file. If you should fail to do this and the router loses power, all of your changes will be lost. The Cisco router will recognize the **copy run start** command in its abbreviated form. Remember that the first part of the command is the action copy, the second part is the "From" location, and the third part is the "To" location.

Because the configuration file used at the router startup is the only file in NVRAM, you do not need to use a file name to copy the file. Configuration files can also be stored in Flash. Because there is more than one file in Flash memory, if you choose to use the startup-config and place configuration files in Flash, you must specify the name of the file.

Because the startup-config can be in stored in different locations, you must use the **boot config** command to specify where the router can find the startup-config at bootup. The default for routers is in NVRAM unless the boot config command is used.

Use the **show running-config** command to view the running configuration file (in RAM). To view the startup configuration file (NVRAM), use the **show startup-config** or ***show config** command.

Initial Configuration mode, also known as the Setup mode, is used when you first set up the router. There are three ways to get into this mode:

- One way is when you first turn on the router.

- Another way is if NVRAM is empty.

- From Privileged mode with the setup command.

Commands for Configuration

Table 5-2 lists the commands for configuration.

Table 5-2: Commands for Configuration

Command	Action
Show startup-config	Shows the configuration that will be loaded when the router boots *or (show config).*
Show running-config	Shows the configuration that is currently loaded into RAM and running.
Erase startup-config	Erases the config in the router's NVRAM and puts you in Setup mode.
Copy running-config	Copies the currently running (active in RAM) configuration file to the startup configuration file.
startup-config	File to the startup configuration file.
Copy startup-config	Copies the startup configuration (NVRAM) to the running-config configuration file. (Used if you make an error in your running-config and want to revert to the startup-config.)
Copy run tftp	Copies the startup-config to a TFTP server. Used for backup purposes. When you use this command, you will be prompted for the TFTP IP address and file name.
Copy tftp run	Copies the config on the TFTP server to the running configuration. Used to restore the router's configuration.

THE CISCO DISCOVERY PROTOCOL

The Cisco Discovery Protocol (CDP) is used by Cisco routers and switches to discover basic information about locally attached and remote devices, routers, and switches. With CDP, you actually learn hardware and protocol information about neighboring devices. You can use this information to troubleshoot and document the network.

- The **show cdp** command will show the two CDP global parameters that can be configured on Cisco devices:
  - **CDP timer** is the frequency that CDP packets are transmitted to all active interfaces.
  - **CDP holdtime** is the amount of time a device will hold packets received from neighbor devices.

The defaults for Cisco routers and switches are sending CDP packets every 60 seconds and a holdtime of 180 seconds. You can use the following commands to change the frequency that CDP packets will be transmitted. You can also see the command to change the CDP holdtime.

> **Router(config)#cdp timer 90*
> Router (config)#**cdp holdtime 240**
> Router(config)#**CTRL+Z**

CDP can be disabled with the **no cdp run** command from Global Configuration mode. **To turn CDP off or on in a router interface, use the no cdp enable and cdp enable commands.*

- The **show cdp neighbors detail** command will give you more detailed information on neighboring devices. CDP packets cannot pass through a Cisco switch, so you only see what is directly attached. For example, if you have a router connected to a switch, you cannot see the other devices connected to the switch.

TELNET

Virtual Terminal Connections (Telnet) is a virtual terminal protocol that allows you to connect to routers remotely instead of having to physically connect to them. I stated previously that you could use the console port to connect to a router, as this is a physical connection. But what if you had hundreds of routers? You can save valuable time if your routers and switches are configured to use Telnet services. The only thing to configure are the VTY passwords, which must be set on each router and switch. Cisco routers can support up to five simultaneous incoming Telnet sessions (vty 0 4).

Since CDP cannot gather information remotely, you can use Telnet to connect to your neighbor devices and then run CDP on the remote devices. You can use the Telnet command from any router prompt as shown below:

RouterB#**telnet 172.16.50.1**
Password: **XXXX**
RouterC>**exit**

NOTE: Instead of using the entire Telnet and IP address command, you can just type the IP address to perform an automatic telnet into the device.

Another time-saving aspect of Telnet is that if you want to keep a connection you've made but then return to the original router, press ***CTRL+SHIFT+6***, release it, and then press **X**. After you complete the key combination, the command prompt is back at the original router.

To view the connections made from your router to a remote device you must use the **show sessions** command.

RouterA#**sh sessions**

NOTE: When you use this command you will notice the asterisk (*) next to one of the connections. This indicates the connection was your last session. You can return to your last session by pressing ENTER twice or enter any session by typing the number of the connection and pressing ENTER twice.

You can list all active connections in use on your router with the show users command.

To end Telnet sessions, type **exit** or **disconnect**. If you want to end the session of a device attached to your router through Telnet, use the clear line # command.

Resolving Hostnames

You can use easy-to-remember hostnames rather than IP addresses for simpler access to
Telnet sessions. In order to use hostnames, however, the router you are using must be
able to translate the hostname to an IP address. The two ways to do this are either to build
a host table on each router or to use a Domain Name System (DNS) server.

Building a Host Table

A host table provides name resolution only on the router it was built on. This means that
if you want to build host tables on your network, you must configure a host table on each
router. If you have many routers you may want to consider using DNS. The **ip host**
command is used as shown below to build a host table:

    Router>**enable**
    Router#**config t**
    Router(config)#**ip host RouterA 172.10.30.2**

The **show hosts** command allows you to view the host table. After using this command
you will notice a Flags column. You will see a **perm** entry, which means it was manually
configured. If it said **temp**, it would be an entry resolved by DNS. You can remove a
hostname with the **no ip host** command as shown below:

    Router>**enable**
    Router#**config t**
    Router(config)#**no ip host RouterA 172.10.30.2**

DNS to Resolve Names

If you have many routers and don't want to create a host table on each router, you can use a DNS server to resolve hostnames. Every time you type a command the router doesn't understand, it tries to resolve this through DNS by default. You can disable the default DNS lookup by using the **no ip domain-lookup** command on your router from Global Configuration mode.

To enable DNS resolution of hostnames, you need to configure the routers to do so:

* The first command is **ip domain-lookup**, which is turned on by default. It needs to be entered only if you previously turned it off.

* The second command is **ip name-server**. This sets the IP address of the DNS server. You can enter the IP address of up to six servers.

* The last command is **ip domain-name**. Although this command is optional, it should be set.

These commands are entered as follows:

    RouterA(config)#**ip domain-lookup**
    RouterA(config)#**ip name-server 172.36.20.2**
    RouterA(config)#**ip domain-name myoffice.com**
    RouterA(config)#**CTRL+Z**

EXAM TIP: Know that the "ip domain-lookup" command enables DNS name resolution, and that "no ip domain-lookup" will turn it off.

1. Which command would be used to configure a router to use hostnames instead of IP addresses?
    a. IP Host
    b. IP Hostname
    c. Name change
    d. DNS name

2. What three sources are used to configure an IOS Cisco device?
    a. Terminal
    b. Server
    c. RAM
    d. NVRAM
    e. TFTP Server

3. Which command would be used to delete the image of a device with an external Flash card?
    a. Erase
    b. Delete
    c. Squeeze
    d. Destroy

4. Which of the following commands is used to load the Cisco IOS from a TFTP server?
    a. copy system tftp ios_filename tftp _address
    b. boot system tftp ios_filename tftp_address
    c. boot system ROM
    d. copy Flash TFTP

5. What is the proper order of sources from which a router will try to load the IOS?
    a. TFTP server, ROM, Flash
    b. ROM, Flash, TFTP server
    c. RAM, TFTP server, ROM
    d. Flash, TFTP server, ROM

6. You are asked to boot the system from a file called "beta" on the network, what command can you use?
   a. copy network beta
   b. copy flash beta
   c. boot network tftp beta (IP address)
   d. boot system beta

7. Which command would you type to copy IOS from a TFTP server to Flash?
   a. copy flash tftp
   b. copy tftp flash
   c. boot flash tftp
   d. boot tftp flash

8. What would you type to copy the contents of Flash to a TFTP server?
   a. copy flash tftp
   b. copy tftp flash
   c. copy ROM flash
   d. copy flash ROM

9. What would you type to view the startup configuration of a router?
   a. view startup-config
   b. run startup-config
   c. show running-config
   d. sh startup-config

10. How do you change the running-config? (Select three.)
    a. config memory
    b. copy tftp running
    c. copy start running
    d. config running-config

11. What are the four areas of ROM microcode?
    a. Bootstrap code
    b. POST code
    c. ROM monitor
    d. Partial IOS
    e. All the above

12. How do you prevent cdp devices from getting information?
    a. RouterA#no cdp run
    b. RouterA(config)# no cdp run
    c. RouterA(config)#disable cdp
    d. RouterA>no cdp run

13. How do you verify and display active Telnet sessions?
    a. RouterA>sh telnet sessions
    b. Router A#sh telnet sessions
    c. RouterA>sh sessions
    d. RouterA#sh sessions

1. **a.** In order to use hostnames, the router you are using must be able to translate the hostname to an IP address. One way to do this is to build a host table on each router. A host table provides name resolution only on the router it was built on. The IP host command is used to build a host table.

2. **a, d, e.** There are three ways or sources to configure an IOS on a Cisco device: the config t command (Terminal), NVRAM, or on the TFTP server.

3. **c.** You can permanently delete the IOS, using the squeeze command.

4. **b.** Enter *boot system tftp ios_filename tftp_ip_address*. Remember that boot system is the command, followed by the location you wish to boot the IOS, the IOS file name, and, finally, the IP address of the TFTP server.

5. **d.** The boot system command is used to change the location of the IOS the system uses at bootup. The router will try to load from Flash, then from the TFTP server, and finally from ROM.

6. **c.** If you need to boot the system from a file on the network called "beta", you would use the following command: boot network tftp beta (IP address).

7. **b.** The new IOS image is copied into the TFTP server's default directory, and then is copied into Flash memory. The command used is *copy tftp flash*, which means *copy* is the command or action to take, *tftp* is where the IOS is copied from, and *flash* is the destination.

8. **a.** The *copy flash tftp* can be used to store your current IOS if the IOS in flash becomes corrupt. This is called backing up your router's IOS. The command means *copy* is the command or action to take, *flash* is where the IOS is copied from, and *tftp* is the destination.

9. **d.** The *show startup-config* or *show config* command is used to view the startup configuration file (NVRAM). IOS can understand abbreviations of commands, such as *sho* or *sh*. This is true of most of the IOS commands. On version 10.3 and earlier, however, you have to write the full command.

10. **a, b, c.** Config memory executes configuration commands stored in NVRAM, and will copy the startup-config to the running-config. Copy tftp run will copy the configuration file on the TFTP server to the running configuration. The copy start run command will copy the startup-config to the running-config.

11. **e.** The four areas of ROM microcode are: bootstrap code, POST code, ROM monitor, and partial IOS.

12. **b.** CDP can be disabled with the *no cdp run* command from Global Configuration mode.

13. **d.** To view the connections made from your router to a remote device you must use the *show sessions* command. IOS can understand abbreviations of commands, such as *sho* or *sh*. This is true of most of the IOS commands. On version 10.3 and earlier, however, you have to write the full command.

Chapter

TCP and the Internet Protocol

These are the areas that are generally testable on the CCNA examination:

1. Network protocols: TCP/IP suite

   • Functions at each layer.

   • Identify the functions of the TCP/IP Transport-layer protocols.

   • Identify the functions of the TCP/IP Network-layer protocols.

   • Identify the functions performed by ICMP.

2. Understand the TCP/IP and DOD models.

3. IP addressing and subnetting:

   • Describe the two parts of a network address.

   • Create a subnet.

4. Know the difference between TCP and UDP.

TCP and the Internet Protocol

Chapter 6

Introduction

There is a lot of information in this chapter. By the time you finish it, you should understand the TCP/IP and DOD models. These models are a condensed version of the OSI model. You will learn to recognize which layer in each model corresponds to the other layer.

TCP is the workhorse of the Internet. It gives reliable data delivery, as well as sequences and provides acknowledgments for the data it transmits. Other important features of TCP include flow control and windowing.

Knowing the differences between TCP and UDP is a must. UDP is not reliable and does not use windowing. It has less overhead, and so it is much quicker than TCP, because UDP does not resend data, provide acknowledgments, or use virtual circuits.

Next you'll learn the functions of ICMP, including hops, Buffers full, TTL, Destination unreachable, and Ping. These are used to ensure that data does not get lost in the network.

Finally, we'll discuss subnetting. When you receive an IP address from InterNIC, it is an address for one network. By using subnetting, you can create mini networks (subnets) that will allow you to utilize routers within the network and all the benefits that go along with them.

TCP/IP AND THE DOD MODEL

The DOD (Department of Defense) model is a condensed version of the OSI model. Its four layers are listed in Table 6-1.

Table 6-1: The TCP/IP and the DOD Model

DOD and TCP/IP Model	*OSI Layers*
Process/Application	Application, Presentation, and Session
Host-to-Host	Transport
Internet	Network
Network Access	Data Link and Physical

- The **Process/Application layer** defines protocols for node-to-node application communication and controls user interface specifications.

- The **Host-to-Host layer** equates to the functions of OSI's Transport layer. It defines protocols used to set up transmission service for applications.

- The **Internet layer** is equivalent to the OSI's Network layer. It designates the protocols used for the transmission of packets over the network as a whole.

- The **Network Access layer** monitors the data exchange between the host and the network.

EXAM TIP: Study the model above and be prepared to recognize which layer in each model corresponds to the other layer.

Table 6-2 lists the DOD model.

Table 6-2: The DOD Model

Process/ Application	Telnet TFTP	FTP SMTP	LPD NFS	SNMP X window
Host-to-Host	TCP	UDP		
*Internet	ICMP IP	BootP	ARP	RARP
Network Access	Ethernet	Fast Ethernet	Token Ring	FDDI

EXAM TIP: Be able to identify which protocols are at each layer, particularly the Internet layer.

FUNCTIONS OF TCP/IP

TCP is a reliable connection-oriented protocol that provides data transfer, multiplexing, error recovery, and flow control using windowing, connection establishment, and termination. The Transport layer is responsible for sequencing the data into the proper order.

- A connection must be established and the two hosts must synchronize each other's initial sequence numbers before communication takes place. This process is called a **three-way handshake**. It is necessary because sequence numbers are not tied to a global clock in the network, and TCP might have a different mechanism for picking the initial sequence number. To achieve reliability, TCP uses sequences, **ACKs (ACKnowledgments)**, and flow control (windowing).

- The TCP window size determines how much data the receiving station will accept at one time before an acknowledgment will be returned. With a window size of 3, three segments will be sent, and one ACK for all three frames will be sent back. No more data may be sent until the segments are ACKed. The starting ACK numbers in TCP are stated during initialization.

- A TCP socket consists of a layer-3 IP address, a layer-4 protocol, and a port number. TCP accomplishes data transfer by establishing a connection between sockets on each of the endpoint computers. Applications use a TCP service by opening a socket, and TCP manages delivery of the data to the other socket. TCP uses the socket connection to perform multiplexing, which is a function used to decide the correct application for a packet based on port number. Applications such as FTP open a socket using a well-known port and listen for connection requests.

Data Transfer

The upper layers use TCP services to control data transfer. A destination IP address, the name of the Transport-layer protocol, and a port number form a socket (i.e. 171.1.1.3, TCP, 23) used to control the transfer of data. TCP achieves data transfer by establishing a connection between a socket on each end of the connection. TCP and UDP have to use port numbers to communicate with the upper layers. Port numbers at the originating source are dynamically assigned a number greater than 1023.

Multiplexing

Servers must use predefined ports so the clients don't need to guess which port to use. These "well-known" port numbers are used by servers: Port 23 for TELNET, port 21 for FTP, port 6 for TCP, port 17 for UDP, and port 80 for HTTP. The client can use any unused port to communicate with a server.

Reliable Data Transfer

Reliable Data Transfer is the most important feature of TCP. TCP does this with the sequence and acknowledgment fields of the header, giving you reliable data transfer for both the sending and receiving machines. TCP segments not received at the other end are resent.

EXAM TIP: It is important to know that TCP sequences and provides acknowledgments for the data it transmits.

Flow Control

TCP flow control also uses sequence and acknowledgment fields, as well as another field called a window.

There are three basic methods of flow control:

- Simple handshake
- Send acknowledgments
- Ensure no data gets lost

Connection Establishment

The first process TCP uses to establish a connection is initializing the sequence and acknowledgment fields and agreeing on which port numbers to use. You could consider this a simple handshake.

The three operational phases in a basic connection-oriented network are:

1. Call setup

2. Data transfer

3. Data segmentation

User Datagram Protocol

User Datagram Protocol (UDP) is not reliable and does not use windowing. Because it has less overhead, UDP is much quicker. UDP does provide data transfer and multiplexing, but does not create a virtual circuit. It also does not contact the destination device before delivering information. Consequently, UDP is considered to be a connectionless protocol. UDP numbers each segment, but does not sequence them. As a matter of fact, UDP does not care in which order the segments arrive at the destination machine.

UDP does not resend data and is usually used when the application itself provides the service. UDP does not use flow control, nor does it establish a connection. UDP just throws the data onto the network and does not care how the data arrives at its destination.

The key attributes you should keep in mind for TCP and UDP are listed in Table 6-3.

Table 6-3: TCP and UDP Key Attributes

TCP	UDP
Virtual circuit	Low overhead
Sequenced	Unsequenced
Acknowledgements	No acknowledgements
Reliable	Unreliable
Connection-oriented	Connectionless
Flow Control	No flow control

EXAM TIP: Study this chart well. A large portion of the exam concentrates on the capabilities of each protocol. Remember: If it sounds like the data transmission is being controlled in any way, then TCP is being used.

Address Resolution Protocol

Address Resolution Protocol (ARP) is used to learn the MAC address of another host, when the IP address is known. Earlier we learned that routing via the IP protocol only sends the data to the router that supports the destination host. When it arrives there, the ARP protocol is used to get the MAC address of the destination host. It actually uses a local broadcast to the LAN segment to learn the information and deliver the data. In more technical terms: An IP packet is sent across a LAN by creating a data-link header and trailer and placing the IP packet between them. At the destination host, the data-link information is stripped off and the original IP packet is processed. **ARP is located in the Network layer of the OSI model, just like IP.** An ARP table is produced, which is a list of MAC addresses mapped to their corresponding IP addresses. While the source address and the destination address (IP addresses) remain constant, the hardware address will change at each router encountered along the packet's route.

Reverse Address Resolution Protocol

Reverse Address Resolution Protocol (RARP), the opposite of ARP, is used when the MAC address is known and you need to learn the IP address. RARP is generally used in a diskless machine, such as a dumb terminal. The machine knows its MAC address (it's on the NIC), but needs an IP address to communicate with other devices on the network. When this type of machine first boots up, the RARP sends out a packet that says "I have a MAC address and I request to learn which IP address is assigned to it." This protocol is not used much because the number of dumb terminal clients shrinks everyday. **RARP is also a Network-layer protocol**.

BootP

BootP stands for Bootstrap Protocol. Like RARP, this protocol is used with diskless workstations to request IP addresses from a BootP server. Again, the client already has a MAC addresses but needs an IP address to communicate. BootP is similar to Microsoft's Dynamic Host Configuration Protocol (DHCP), which provides clients with not only an IP address, but also a subnet mask, default gateway information, and the locations of the DNS and WINS servers.

Internet Control Message Protocol

Internet Control Message Protocol (ICMP) performs its functions in the Network layer (layer 3) and is used in conjunction with IP. In fact, all TCP/IP hosts use ICMP for the following reasons: ICMP is primarily used by gateways or destination hosts to inform them of certain network problems. ICMP is like a management protocol and messaging service provider for IP. The functions that ICMP performs include:

- *Destination unreachable:* Any time a router can't send an IP datagram to its final destination, it uses ICMP to send a message back to the sender informing them of the problem.

- *Buffer full:* ICMP will also send a message when the router's memory buffer is full and can't process any more incoming datagrams. Basically, the message says "stop transmitting and give me time to process what is currently in my memory buffer." These messages are called source-quench messages.

- ***Hops:** Every network determines the maximum number of routers an IP datagram is allowed to go through. Each router that the datagram is processed through is called a hop. A maximum number of hops is created to prevent routing loops. When a packet reaches its hop limit, the last router to receive that datagram deletes it. That router will then use ICMP to send a message notifying the sender of the packet's deletion.

- ***Ping: Packet Internet Groper uses ICMP echo messages to check the physical connectivity of machines on a network. You can also use the Trace command.** You could say that the Ping attribute of ICMP provides network testing and verification. Here is an example of a Ping to a network server: Ping 145.43.23.2. This command is performed at a DOS prompt. If the Ping is successful the connection is OK. If the Ping is not successful then you would check the cabling and NIC card to ensure proper connectivity.

- **Time to live (TTL):** TTL is an ICMP message from a router to a sending host informing it that the TTL was exceeded and the packet was discarded. TTL works with the maximum number of hops to help eliminate loops. If either of the two occur, the packet will be discarded.

- **Traceroute:** Traceroute also uses ICMP to find a path the packet takes as it goes through a network.

EXAM TIP: Learn the functions of ICMP. First, read all the functions, then concentrate on the highlighted items. The exam may use different terms, but if you learn their functions you should be well on your way to passing the exam.

These are the areas that are generally testable on the CCNA examination:

IP addressing and subnetting:

- Describe the two parts of a network address.
- Create a subnet.

IP ADDRESSING TERMS AND CONCEPTS

- **Unique IP Address:** Each host should have a unique IP address to communicate. If the IP address is not unique, one of the two users with the same IP address will be denied network access to resources. An IP address contains a total of 32 bits, which are then divided into four octets (8 bits each). Here is a typical example: 172.34.25.14

- **Logical Addressing:** IP addresses are a logical addressing scheme, not a physical one, allowing for future growth. IP is also responsible for identifying a path to a network by a process called route determination.

- **Numerical Grouping:** IP addresses are grouped numerically. This means that you can subnet your network with numerical grouping. You will learn much more about subnetting later.

- **Network Address:** All hosts on the network must use the same network address. If they don't, they will not be able to communicate with the local network.

- **Subnets:** Breaking a network down into smaller more manageable networks creates what are known as subnets. Users in the same subnet must be attached to the same medium (cable) and not be separated by a router. If a router did separate the users on the same subnet, it would require two separate router interfaces, therefore requiring two network (subnet) addresses.

- **IP Networks:** There are five classes of networks: A, B, C, D, and E. In Table 6-4, however, we will only cover the first four classes. Remember that each computer will have the same network address (i.e. 128.14.0.0 Class B). The host portion will be unique for each host.

Table 6-4: Network Classes

Network Address Bits Used	Type Class	Address Bit Range	Default Mask	Leading Bit
8 bits	Class A	1-126	255.0.0.0	0
16 bits	Class B	128-191	255.255.0.0	10
*24 bits	Class C	192-223	255.255.255.0	110
	*Class D	224-239	Used for multicasting	
	Class E	240-255	Used for experimental/research	

NOTE: You may notice that network address 127 is missing. It is used to perform the Ping command and therefore cannot be used as a network address. Another number that cannot be used is 255, which is used as a broadcast address. A typical broadcast address for a Class C network would be 0.0.0.255.

NOTE: Normally, you will see IP addresses combined with their default mask, such as a Class C IP address like: 192.16.10.4, 255.255.255.0. But there are some possible test questions that will give you a Class B IP address and try to trick you with a Class C subnet mask. Don't fall for this trick, because it does have the default subnet mask of 255.255.0.0, but in addition the third octet is used to subnet the local network and appears like a Class C address.

Examples of network addresses with the default mask are listed in Table 6-5.

Table 6-5: Network Addresses with the Default Mask

Class Type	Network Number	Default Mask
A	15.0.0.0	255.0.0.0
B	129.15.0.0	255.255.0.0
C	192.12.12.0	255.255.255.0

SUBNETTING

Many people have difficulty calculating subnets. In the real world you will use a subnetting chart instead of manually calculating a subnet mask. But the exam includes subnet questions that require you to manually figure out the answer.

I have developed a surefire way to calculate subnets in seconds. I will start out with the traditional formulas before describing my own method.

Subnetting Overview

- Subnetting extends the network portion of the address to let a single network be logically divided into sections (subnets). Routers look at each of these subnets as distinct networks, and will route among them. This helps in managing large networks by isolating traffic between portions. IP performs a bitwise ANDing process to determine local and remote networks. A subnet/network number is the lowest value numerically in that network or subnet (for example: 192.168.100.0). All subnet numbers have binary 0s for the host part of the subnet number. It is common for groups of hosts to communicate routinely with each other, and to communicate less outside the group. When logically subnetting a network, the network resources, geographic distances, and communication patterns need to be considered in order for the network to operate efficiently. To subnet a network, we add one or more bits to the default subnet mask, thus reducing the number of bits for the host address.

- **A broadcast address is an address that exists in IP containing all 1s (FF.FF.FF.FF)**. This address is reserved for an IP broadcast into that network. All hosts on that subnet will receive this packet. Broadcast addresses address all devices on a LAN. A multicast address is a type of packet destined for a specific set of networks. A unicast address addresses an individual LAN interface card. The purpose of the subnet mask is to borrow bits from the host field and designate them as the subnet field.

IP Addressing Rules

Neither the network address, host address, nor subnet portion of an IP address can be set to "all binary zeros" or "all binary ones".

The network 127.x.x.x is reserved as a loop-back address for testing protocol stack and cannot be used as a network address.

For IP communication, the minimum information required is an IP address and an associated subnet mask. A subnet mask is used to determine the network ID and host ID from the IP address.

- **Subnet masks:** A subnet mask is used to define the number of bits that will be used to subnet. The remaining bits are then used to define the number of host bits in an address.

- **Subnet/network address:** A subnet/network number is the lowest numeric value that is used to identify that network or subnet. The IP address you receive from InterNIC is for one network only. In order to use routers and to make your network more manageable, you have to steal bits from the host address portion to break your network into subnets. You are given only one 32-bit address and, depending on the class, you may not be able to use many host bits for subnetting.

There are two numbers that cannot be used in subnetting. One is "0", the network address, which tells the router that these octets are used for the network address. The other is "255", the broadcast address used to send messages to every host on the network or subnet. You can assign individual host addresses between these addresses. *A broadcast address is an address that can be displayed as FF.FF.FF.FF.*

EXAM TIP: Be able to determine that FF.FF.FF.FF, 128.24(.255.255), and 00000000.00000000 (.11111111.11111111) all are the same. Learn the three different ways to display a broadcast address.

IP Subnetting

Subnetting is the process of creating subdivisions of a single Class A, B, or C network, and treating the subnet as if it were a network itself. There are two reasons to use subnets rather than a different class network:

- IP grouping requires that hosts in the same group not be separated by a router. Therefore, they need their own network/subnet identifier for use in routing.

- IP routing requires that hosts separated by a router must be in a different group (subnet).

NOTE: If you have a small network with no future plans for growth, subnetting would not be used. However, if growth is expected, as in most networks today, you must subnet your network.

Subnet Attributes

- Members in one subnet all have the same subnet address (network address).
- Members of one subnet cannot be separated by a router.
- Members of a second subnet must be separated from the first by a router.

Subnetting Simplified

Network addresses and subnet addresses operate like ZIP codes. The Post Office sends your mail to a ZIP code (network address). Your home address is the same as the host address. Mail is delivered to your neighborhood post office according to ZIP code, then delivered to your home (host address).

Benefits of Subnetting

- Subnetting reduces network traffic. Remember that when you subnet, there must be a router in between. Routers can then be used to keep traffic on its own segment.
- Network performance is optimized, because of the reduced network traffic on each subnet.
- Management is simplified. It's easier to troubleshoot, identify, and isolate network problems in a smaller subnet than in a larger network.
- Geographical distances are overcome. For example, two locations can be in the same network when you subnet. Subnetting lets you create separate networks with routers in between, allowing communication with each other.

Implementing Subnetting

Before you can subnet you must determine the number of required network IDs (subnets):

- One network ID is required for each subnet.

- One network ID is required for each Wide Area Network connection.

Next you must determine the number of required host IDs per subnet. In other words, you must know how many hosts will be on each subnet:

- One host ID is required for each TCP/IP host. That is because each host needs a unique IP address to communicate on the network.

- One host ID for each router interface.

Subnetting: The Actual Process

Subnetting is the process of creating little subnetworks from a single, larger network. The network address will remain the same, while the host portion is used to create the subnet. Networks do not need to have subnets and use the default subnet mask.

The Traditional Model

The first step to subnetting is determining the number of subnets needed, followed by the number of hosts per subnet.

Maximum Number of Subnets

Formula: 2 (to the power of number of masked bits in subnet mask) –2 = number of subnets

We start with a base 2 (binary), then figure to the power of masked-out bits (or in layman's terms, the number of 1s in the binary form of the subnet mask). For example, let's look at a Class B subnet mask of 255.255.192.0, which is 11111111.11111111.11000000.00000000 in binary. The number of masked-out bits in this number is 2. We get that from counting the 1s in the binary representation of 192 (11000000). At this point we have 2 to the power of 2, which is 4. For the last step, we then subtract 2 from that number. So for this example, the maximum number of subnets would be 2.

Maximum Number of Host ID's per Subnet

Formula: 2(to the power of number of unmasked bits in subnet mask) –2 = number of host ID's

Once again, we start with a base 2 (binary), then figure to the power of unmasked bits (or in layman's terms, the number of 0s in the binary form of the subnet mask). For example, let's look at that Class B subnet mask of 255.255.192.0 again, which is 11111111.11111111.11000000.00000000 in binary. The number of unmasked bits in this number is 14. We get that from counting the 0's in 11000000.00000000 (the binary representation of 192.0). At this point, we have 2 to the power of 14, which is 16,384. For the last step, we then subtract 2 from that number. So for this example, the maximum number of host IDs would be 16,382.

My Method

I divide the subnetting into a four-step process.

- **Step 1 – Number of Subnets.** The first step is to determine the number of subnets. I like to use a standard binary chart to complete each step. This is what it looks like:

128	64	32	16	8	4	2	1
0	0	0	0	0	0	0	0

The numbers at the top represent the value of each bit. For our first example, let's say you need 6 subnets. You have to determine the number of bits you will steal from the host portion. Starting from the right side of the chart, add the numbers at the top until you reach the required amount.

NOTE: Any time you count from the right do not count the number 1. This is because you cannot use the numbers 0 and 1 in IP addressing. Not counting the last bit mathematically excludes these numbers.

Calculation Chart	IP Address Example
128 64 32 16 8 4 2 1	192.30.5.0
0 0 0 0 0 1 1 1 (fourth octet)	.11100000

Notice that to reach 6 subnets you need to use 3 bits from the host address. Just add the numbers at the top, except for the 1 column: $4 + 2 = 6$. During the exam this process will take seconds to perform. Again, when you perform calculation from the right, don't add the 1.

- **Step 2 – Number of Hosts.** The second step is to determine the number of hosts. Since you have already established how many bits are used for subnetting, the remaining bits are used for hosts. This is a set number because, in this case, there are only 8 total bits and three are used for subnetting. That leaves 5 bits for possible hosts. If 5 bits is not enough to support the number of hosts on the subnet, then you have to reduce the number of bits for subnetting. Now, let's use those 5 bits counting from the right and add the numbers at the top. Don't count the one.

Calculation Chart	IP Address Example
128 64 32 16 8 4 2 1	192.30.5.0
0 0 0 1 1 1 1 1 (fourth octet)	.00011111

The number of hosts per subnet should be clear to you. Add the numbers $2+4+8+16$ for a total of 30. In this example you can have 6 subnets with 30 hosts per subnet. I believe this is easier than the traditional way.

- **Step 3 – Subnet Mask.** Given a default mask of 255.255.255.0, the subnet mask is applied to the fourth octet, telling devices like routers or computers that subnetting is taking place (i.e., 255.255.255.224). You would use the default at each client's computer. In this step you use the same three bits that you subnetted with and apply them from the left, then count all the numbers at the top. In this example (128+64+32) the subnet mask is 224.

Calculation Chart	IP Address Example
128 64 32 16 8 4 2 1	192.30.5.0
1 1 1 0 0 0 0 0 (fourth octet)	.11100000

- **Step 4 – Subnet or Network ID.** This step separates each subnet with its own subnet identification. Again, use the three bits you used for subnetting and apply them to the chart. Starting from the left, the last number of the last bit (the farthest to the right) represents your first network ID. In this case it is 32.

Calculation Chart	IP Address Example
128 64 32 16 8 4 2 1	192.30.5.0
1 1 1 0 0 0 0 0 (fourth octet)	.11100000

Creating IP Host Ranges

Now that you have your first network ID (32), we can create the remaining five subnets by adding the initial ID to itself. For example: 32 + 32 = 64, so 64 is the next ID. Add 32 to the result again and again until you have all six subnets. Here are the six subnet IDs:

- 32
- 64
- 96
- 128
- 160
- 192

Next, we can create the IP host ranges. On subnet 32, you start the next available IP address at 33 and continue to 62.

NOTE: 63 is not used. That is because 63 is now the broadcast number for that subnet.

On subnet 32 of our example, you can use the numbers 33 or 63. You may lose addresses when you subnet. Table 6-6 shows what the IP address range looks like for our subnet 32.

Table 6-6: IP Address Range

Subnet ID	Usable Hosts	Broadcast Address
32	33-62	63

Continue with the other five subnets.

NOTE: The broadcast address for the previous subnet is one less than the next subnet ID.

All the subnet IDs and their usable host addresses are shown in Table 6-7.

Table 6-7: Subnet IDs and Their Usable Host Addresses

Subnet ID	Usable Hosts	Broadcast Address
32	33-62	63
64	65-94	95
96	97-126	127
128	129-158	159
160	161-190	191
192	193-222	223

It is simple to identify the subnet ID and the broadcast address, then fill in the hosts. You can apply the calculation chart to all three network classes.

Apply What You Learned

Plan a network: IP subnet design with a Class C network.

You will need 4 sites (subnets), one Ethernet at each site. Choose a mask that will maximize the number of hosts per subnet. Use a network address of 193.1.1.0

Answer: 255.255.255.224

RECAP

When doing your calculations, start on the right for subnet and host calculations, but from the left for subnet mask and subnet ID, as shown in Table 6-8. If you can remember this, then subnetting will not give you any problems.

Table 6-8: Calculation Chart

	Subnet Mask Subnet ID							#s of Subnets #s of Hosts
	128	64	32	16	8	4	2	1
(Left) (Right)								
	1	1	1	0	0	0	0	0

IP Addressing

An IP address is a 32-bit address broken down into four blocks of 8 bits represented by a decimal number, as depicted in Table 6-9. For example, the dotted-decimal IP address 207.56.10.3 represents the binary number 11001111.00111000.00001010.00000011.

Table 6-9: IP Addressing

Class	Format	Leading Bit Pattern	Decimal Range of First Byte of Network Address	Maximum Networks	Maximum Hosts per Network
A	Net.Node.Node.Node	0	1-127	127	16,777,214
B	Net.Net.Node.Node	10	128-191	16,384	65,534
C	Net.Net.Net.Node	110	192-223	2,097,152	254

Exclusions to IP Addressing

Table 6-10 lists the exclusions to IP addressing.

Table 6-10: Subnet IDs and Their Usable Host Address

Network address of all 0s	Interpreted to mean "this network or segment"	Example: (0).5.154.10 (Class A)
Network address of all 1s	Interpreted to mean "all networks"	Example: (255).5.154.10 (Class A)
Network 127	Reserved for loopback tests	Example: (127).0.0.0
Node address of all 0s	Interpreted to mean "this node"	Example: 123.(0.0.0) (Class A)
Node address of all 1s	Interpreted to mean "all nodes" on the specified network	Example: 123.(255.255.255) (Class A)
Entire IP address set to 0s	Used by Cisco routers to designate the default route	Example: 0.0.0.0
Entire IP address set to 1s	Broadcast to all nodes on the current network	Example: 255.255.255.255

Subnetting is depicted in Table 6-11.

Table 6-11: Subnetting

Class	Format	Default Subnet Mask
A	Net.Node.Node.Node	255.0.0.0
B	Net.Net.Node.Node	255.255.0.0
C	Net.Net.Net.Node	255.255.255.0

1. In the TCP/IP model, the Internet layer maps to which OSI layer or layers?
   a. Transport
   b. Network
   c. Session
   d. Data Link

2. In the TCP/IP model the Process/Application layer maps to which OSI layer or layers? (Select all that apply.)
   a. Application
   b. Transport
   c. Presentation
   d. Session
   e. Network

3. Which of the following is the Internet layer protocol in the TCP/IP stack?
   a. TCP
   b. UDP
   c. IP
   d. SPX

4. What are the three basic methods of flow control?
   a. Simple handshake
   b. Doesn't care if data gets lost
   c. Ensure no data gets lost
   d. Doesn't send acknowledgements
   e. Sends acknowledgements

5. What protocol is used to obtain a MAC address from a known IP address?
   a. ARP
   b. RARP
   c. ICMP
   d. TCP

6. What two commands are used to troubleshoot a network connection?
   a. IPCONFIG
   b. CONFIG
   c. PING
   d. TRACE

7. Which class allows for the fewest usable hosts?
   a. Class C
   b. Class D
   c. Class E
   d. Class A
   e. Class B

8. You have an IP address of 192.114.36.10. Identify the network class and the subnet mask that would provide for at least 14 hosts per subnet.
   a. Class B, 255.255.240.0
   b Class C, 255.255.255.240
   c. Class C, 255.255.255.224
   d. Class C, 255.255.255.248

9. What is the correct subnet mask for the address 209.76.25.1 /26?
   (**NOTE:** The /26 means there are 26 active bits in the combination of the network address and subnet addresses, which can be transformed to 11111111.11111111.11111111.11000000)
   a. 255.255.255.192
   b. 255.255.255.224
   c. 255.255.255.240
   d. 255.255.255.248

10. What is the correct network address for the host 209.76.25.72 /26?
    a. 209.76.25.32
    b. 209.76.25.16
    c. 209.76.25.8
    d. 209.76.25.64

11. What is the correct broadcast address for the host 172.16.64.128 using a mask of 255.255.192.0?
    a. 172.16.126.0
    b. 172.16.64.0
    c. 172.16.127.0
    d. 172.26.191.0

12. Which of the following is an invalid host address using a subnet mask of 255.255.255.192?
    a. 10.1.1.65
    b. 10.1.1.127
    c. 10.1.1.126
    d. 10.1.1.120

13. Which of the following is the valid host range for the IP address 192.168.168.188 255.255.255.192?
    a. 192.168.168.128-191
    b. 192.168.168.129-191
    c. 192.168.168.127-191
    d. 192.168.168.129-190

14. Given an IP address of 172.16.10.50 and a subnet mask of 255.255.255.0, which of the following is the correct network and host address?
    a. 172.16.10.0 (network) 0.0.0.50 (host)
    b. 172.16.0.0 (network) 0.0.10.50 (host)
    c. 172.0.0.0 (network) 0.16.10.50 (host)
    d. 0.0.16.10 (network) 172.16.0.0 (host)

15. Given an IP address of 172.16.126.0 and a subnet mask of 255.255.192.0, which of the following is the correct subnet ID?
    a. 128
    b. 64
    c. 32
    d. 192

16. Given an IP address of 172.16.126.0 and a subnet mask of 255.255.192.0, which of the following is the correct IP address range for this IP address?
    a. 64-127
    b. 64-126
    c. 65-126
    d. 64-128

17. What is the protocol and purpose of the following address: 238.255.255.255?
    a. IPX, a SAP broadcast
    b. 10, a multiple cost
    c. IP, a multicast address
    d. IP, a direct broadcast
    e. IPX, a flooded broadcast

18. Which three are typical operational phases in a basic connection-oriented network?
    a. Call setup
    b. Data transfer
    c. Load balancing
    d. Call transmission
    e. Call filterization
    f. Data segmentation
    g. Data link identification

19. How many valid hosts IP addresses are available on the subnet 176.12.44.16/30?
    a. 2 hosts
    b. 16,553 hosts
    c. 14 hosts
    d. 254 hosts

20. Which layer does ICMP belongs to?
    a. Transport layer
    b. Data Link layer
    c. Network layer
    d. Session layer

TCP and the Internet Protocol　　　　　　　　　　　　**137**

21. Which of the following statements about ICMP is correct?
   a. Only IPX/SPX hosts implement ICMP.
   b. Only some TCP/IP hosts implement the ICMP.
   c. Only the hosts designated by the administrator implement the ICMP.
   d. All TCP/IP hosts implement the ICMP.

22. What is a characteristic of connection-oriented communication?
   a. It provides fast but unreliable delivery of datagrams.
   b. It provides assurance of packet delivery.
   c. It uses store-and-forward techniques to move datagrams between computers.
   d. It uses message-oriented communication for processing e-mail.

23. Choose the correct definitions matching the Transport layer: (Select three.)
   a. TCP - Provides flow control and error checking
   b. TCP - Provides connectionless datagram service
   c. UDP - Provides connectionless datagram service
   d. TCP - Provides connection-oriented services
   e. UDP - Provides connection-oriented services
   f. UDP - Provides flow control and error checking

24. Which of the following protocols is a Transport-layer protocol that establishes a virtual circuit before transmitting and is connection-oriented?
   a. IP
   b. ICMP
   c. TCP
   d. UDP
   e. IPX

25. In which type of communication does the receiving computer send an acknowledgement back to the source after a packet has been received?
   a. UDP - Connection-oriented
   b. TCP - Connection-oriented
   c. UDP - Connectionless
   d. TCP - Connectionless

26. Which of the following are features of connection-oriented transmissions? (Select all that apply.)
    a. Reliability
    b. Slower communication
    c. Faster communication
    d. If packets are not received they are resent
    e. Sequencing
    f. Packets are not resent

27. When using a connection-oriented type of communication, which OSI layer's protocols are responsible for sequencing the data into the proper order?
    a. Network
    b. Session
    c. Transport
    d. Data Link

28. Which of the following are features of connectionless transmissions? (Select all that apply.)
    a. Little or no reliability
    b. Reliability
    c. Slower communication
    d. Faster communication
    e. Packets are not resent
    f. Packets are resent

29. Connection-oriented service involves what three phases?
    a. Establish the connection
    b. Transfer the data
    c. Terminate the connection
    d. All the above

30. Choose the correct definitions matching the Network layer. (Select two.)
    a. IP - Route determination
    b. IP - Virtual circuit
    c. ICMP - Provides sequencing
    d. ICMP - Provides network testing and verification
    e. TCP - Reliable
    f. UCP - Unreliable

31. What command sets up a secondary IP address of 192.15.1.7 with a class C subnet mask?
    a. ip secondary ip address 192.15.1.7 255.255.255.0
    b. ip secondary 192.15.1.7 255.255.255.0 ip address
    c. ip address 192.15.1.7 255.255.255.0 secondary
    d. ip address 192.15.1.7 secondary

Answers and Explanations

1. **b.** The Internet layer is equivalent to the OSI's Network layer. It designates the protocols used in the transmission of packets over the network as a whole.

2. **a. c, d.** In the TCP/IP and DOD models, the Process/Application layer defines protocols for node-to-node application communication and controls user interface specifications and maps to the OSI layers: Application, Presentation, and Session.

3. **c.** The Internet-layer protocol in the TCP/IP stack holds the IP protocol. Some of the other protocols located here are ICMP, ARP, RARP, and BootP.

4. **a, c, e.** The three basic methods of flow control are a simple handshake, ensure no data gets lost, and sends acknowledgements.

5. **a.** Earlier we learned that routing via the IP protocol only sends the data to the router that supports the destination host. When it arrives there, the ARP protocol is used to get the MAC address of the destination host. It actually uses a local broadcast to the LAN segment to learn the information and deliver the data.

6. **c, d.** Packet Internet Groper uses ICMP echo messages to check the physical connectivity of machines on a network. You can also use the Trace command.

7. **a.** Class C has the fewest maximum hosts per network.

8. **b.** The first octet of the given IP address is 192, which is in the range of Class C. (See Table 6-9 for more information.) $14 = 2^4 - 2$, which means the last byte of its subnet mask should have four 0s in the binary form and four 1s at the left side for masking. $128 + 64 + 32 + 16 = 240$. Therefore the network mask is 255.255.255.240.

9. **a.** You know the Class is C from the first octet of the address, which means only the last octet can be used for subnetting and the first three octets (24 bits) are used for the network address. It leaves 2 bits for subnetting. Now take those 2 bits and apply them to my Calculation Chart (from the left). Add the two decimal values together and that is your answer: $128 + 64 = 192$.

10. **d.** Using 2 bits from the host portion, apply these bits to the Calculation Chart and the last number becomes the network identification address. In this case the number is 64.

11. **c.** The mask number 192 tells you that 2 bits are used to subnet. Apply these 2 bits to the Calculation Chart, and 64 is the network ID. Now you go one step further and add 64 + 64 = 128 for the next network ID. 64 (network ID) 65-126 (usable IP address) 127 (Network Broadcast). Therefore the answer is 127.

12. **b.** The mask number 192 tells you that 2 bits are used to subnet. Apply these 2 bits to the Calculation Chart, and 64 is the network ID. Now you go one step further and add 64 + 64 = 128 for the next network ID. 64 (network ID) 65-126 (usable IP addresses) 127 (network broadcast). Because network ID 64 has a usable address range from 65-126, 10.1.1.127 could not be a valid answer since it is the broadcast address for this segment.

13. **d.** You are using 2 bits to subnet. Identify the network ID of 64, then figure out the ranges such as: 64 (network ID) 65-126 (usable IP addresses) 127 (network broadcast). But because the answer choices are in the network address, figure out the network address 128 (network ID) 129-190 (usable IP addresses) 191 (network broadcast).

14. **a.** Take the mask 255.255.255 that represents the network address, and the rest represents the host address. Apply this to the given IP address to determine the host address.

15. **b.** The subnet mask of 192 means you used 2 bits to subnet. Apply the bits to the Calculation Chart from the left. The last bit number is the subnet ID of 64.

16. **c.** The mask number 192 tells you that 2 bits are used to subnet. Apply these 2 bits to the Calculation Chart, and 64 is the network ID. Now you go one step further and add 64+64=128 for the next network ID. 64 (network ID) 65-126 (usable IP addresses) 127 (network broadcast). Therefore the answer is 65-126.

17. **c.** If you refer to Table 6-4, you will see that an IP address 238 falls in the range of 224-239 of the Class D used for multicasting.

18. **a, b, f.** The three operational phases in a basic connection-oriented network: call setup, data transfer, and data segmentation.

19. **a.** /30 means that there are 30 1s in the combination of the network address and subnet bits, which is 11111111.11111111.11111111.11111100. Notice the two zeros at the end. This means two bits were used for hosts. Now apply these bits to my chart from the right and don't count the first bit from the right. The number should be 2.

20. **c.** Internet Control Message Protocol (ICMP) performs its functions in the Network layer (layer 3) and is used in conjunction with IP.

21. **d.** Internet Control Message Protocol (ICMP) performs its functions in the Network layer (layer 3) and is used in conjunction with IP. In fact, all TCP/IP hosts use ICMP for the following reasons: ICMP is primarily used by gateways or destination hosts to inform them of certain network problems. ICMP is like a management protocol and messaging service provider for IP.

22. **b.** A connection-oriented protocol provides data transfer, multiplexing, error recovery, and flow control using windowing, connection establishment, and termination. Error control would provide assurance of packet delivery.

23. **a, c, d.** TCP is a reliable connection-oriented protocol that provides data transfer, multiplexing, error recovery, and flow control using windowing, connection establishment, and termination. User Datagram Protocol (UDP) is not reliable and does not use windowing. Because it has less overhead, UDP is much quicker than TCP. UDP does not contact the destination device before delivering information. Because of this, UDP considered a connectionless protocol.

24. **c.** TCP establishes a virtual circuit before transmitting and is connection-oriented.

25. **b.** Using the connection-oriented TCP service, the receiving computer sends an acknowledgement back to the source after a packet has been received.

26. **a, b, d.** TCP uses sequences, ACKs, and flow control to ensure reliability. TCP segments not received at the other end are resent. Because of these features, it has more overhead than UDP and carries a slower communication.

27. **c.** The Transport layer is responsible for sequencing the data into the proper order.

28. **a, d, e.** Connectionless transmission is not reliable and does not use windowing. Because it has fewer overheads, it is much quicker. It does not resend data if packets are not received.

29. **d.** Connection-oriented protocol provides data transfer, multiplexing, error recovery, and flow control using windowing, connection establishment, and termination.

30. **a, d.** IP is responsible for identifying a path to a network by a process called route determination. ICMP performs its functions in the Network layer and is used in conjunction with IP. ICMP is primarily used by gateways or destination hosts to inform them of certain network problems.

31. **c.** *ip address 192.15.1.7 255.255.255.0 secondary* will set up a secondary IP address of 192.15.1.7 with a Class C subnet mask.

Chapter 7

IP Routing

These are the areas that are generally testable on the CCNA examination:

1. Understand the IP routing process.

2. Create and verify static routing.

3. Create and verify default routing.

4. Resolve network loops in distance-vector routing protocols.

5. Configure and verify RIP routing.

6. Configure and verify IGRP routing.

Introduction

IP routing is done on Cisco routers. In this chapter you will learn how to build static (manual) and dynamic (RIP, IGRP) routing tables. There are definite advantages and disadvantages to a routing table built with static and dynamic methods. You will also learn how to designate a default route.

Next, you will learn how to activate a router's interface by using the **IP address** command. You must use the **no shut** command to turn on the interface.

You will also learn important aspects of distance-vector routing protocols, and exactly what they can do. You will learn that these protocols are dynamic, meaning they will automatically build routing tables. The defaults of RIP and IGRP will be covered.

The next topic to be discussed will be "counting to infinity," an important problem with distance-vector routing protocols. The solutions to counting to infinity are: maximum hop count, split horizon, poison reverse, route poisoning, triggered updates, and hold-downs.

Finally, you will learn how to enable RIP on a router with the **router rip** and **network** commands. You must know how to enable IGRP on your router with the **router igrp** command followed by the autonomous system number. You will then use the **network** command followed by the network address.

THE IP ROUTING PROCESS

Every router has a routing table, built either manually or dynamically. The routing table is used to identify a path to a different network by comparing the packet's destination address to this table. This path is then used to send data from a host on one network to a host on another network. If the packet's destination address does not match an entry in the routing table, the packet is sent to the router's default route address. If the default gateway is not identified, the packet is simply discarded.

I think I can make the process easier to understand. Before the routing decision is made, the sending host must check the packet's destination address. This will determine if the destination host is on the same subnet. If it is, the packet will not be routed. But if it is not on the same segment, then it must be routed. *Next, the sending host must learn the hardware address of the default gateway. ARP is used for this purpose. After ARP receives the hardware address, the packet can be sent to the default gateway.* If the default gateway has a route entry in its routing table, the packet is sent to the next router, where the whole process starts over again until the packet reaches its final destination.

STATIC, DEFAULT, AND DYNAMIC ROUTING

We will now look at the three ways that routing tables can be built. Without a routing table the packets will just be discarded. Routing tables store the different routes to other segments in your network. When these tables are built manually by an administrator, they are called static routes. Routing tables can also be dynamically built and maintained by routing protocols, something to consider if you have many routers. When the router is first turned on, it knows only the paths to subnets that are directly connected to it.

Static Routing

Remember that even a static route is set up manually. You must use special care while doing so, because one little typo could affect your whole network. The first step in setting up a static route is to assign an IP address to the interface, followed by the **no shutdown** command. This command is absolutely necessary, because this is what actually activates the interface. This command would look like the following:

Router>**en**   (User level)
Router#**config t**   (Privileged level)
Router(Config)#**interface e0**   (Global config level)
Router(Config-if)#**ip address 192.30.20.1 255.255.255.0**   (Interface level)
Router(Config-if)#**no shut**. (Interface level)

> **EXAM TIP: Look at these commands and understand at which level the command is being performed. Know the "IP address" command and that after that command, you put the interface's IP address followed by a subnet mask. (The example is using a default mask.) Finally, know that you must use the "no shut" command to turn on the interface.**

The biggest problem with static routing tables is that they must be built and updated manually. On the positive side, a static route allows your routers to limit access to the network. This is a good security feature, that allows users access only to the resources that you choose. Another benefit of static routes is bandwidth conservation. This is

because you are not using dynamic routing protocols, which use up bandwidth to communicate route updates. Static routes are usually used when routing from a network to a stub network (a network with a single route). Static routes are built with the *"ip route" command. Below is what each item in a static route means:

Ip route/network/mask/address/interface (distance)
          1   2   3   4   5

1. **Destination Network:** The network address of the destination network or subnet

2. **Mask:** Subnet mask

3. **Next Hop Address:** IP address of the next hop router

4. **Exit Interface:** Used instead of the next hop address (does not work on an Ethernet LAN)

5. **Administrative Distance:** Static routes have a default of 1 (can be changed by putting a different number here)

EXAM TIP: You must know not only the "ip route" command, but also what each of the entries means. Usually you will only be required to know the first three entries, but you may have to know the fifth one.

* *IP route* *192.30.20.0*   *255.255.255.0*   *192.30.20.2*
           1   2   3

NOTE: The static route shown above is a typical example of an Ethernet network. Don't worry about items 4 and 5.

Benefits of Static Routing

- Very little or no overhead on the router's CPU: Well, that is only partially true because the packet must still be processed through the router, but the CPU is not being used to build and maintain the routing table.

- No bandwidth usage between routers: Again, this refers to the bandwidth saved due to information not being passed to each router to build and maintain routing tables.

- Security: The administrator determines who will have access to which resources.

Disadvantages of Static Routing

- You must really know the layout of your network because one incorrect entry in a routing table can create problems in your network. You should make a map of your network identifying all the routers and which route you would like to build.

- If your network is always growing, every time a router is added to the network, you will have to manually make the updates to each router on the network.

- If your network is too large, just maintaining static routes would be overwhelming.

NOTE: The administrative distance is a rating of the source's trustworthiness expressed in a numeric value from 0-255. The higher the number, the lower the trustworthiness rating. For example, the rating for RIP networks is 120. Directly connected routes have a rating of 0 and static routes have a rating of 1. This means the router will use directly connected routes first, then static routes, and then any other routes that are in the routing table. In this case, RIP routes would be checked next.

EXAM TIP: Know the benefits of static routing: little or no overhead on the router's CPU, no bandwidth usage between routers, and increased security. Also, know the disadvantages: incorrect entries can cause problems; each time a router is added you must manually update all the network's routers; and if your network is too large it would take too much time to maintain static routes.

Showing IP Routes

When finished configuring your router with static routes, you can review them with the "*show running-config*" and "*show ip route*" commands. Because static routes are manually configured, you should test each route (with the Ping command). Be very careful when typing static routes.

NOTE: When you use one of the two above commands, take a good look at the routing table. The "S" in the first column of the route table stands for static entries. These have an administrative trustworthiness of 1. Now look at another entry, such as one that starts with a "C". The "C" means that the route is directly connected and has a priority of 0.

Configuring IP Routes

Previously, I gave you the steps to configure an IP route. The example below is the same, but with the addition of two commands at the end. The CTRL+Z will place you back into Privileged mode and will set you up to perform the next command. Next, type "copy run start" to copy the running configuration into the startup-config. If you don't do this, the IP routes you made would be lost. Don't let all your hard work go to waste.

    RouterA#**config t**
    RouterA(config)#**ip route 172.16.30.0   255.255.255.0   172.16.20.2**
    RouterA(config)#**CTRL+Z**
    RouterA#**copy run start**

> **EXAM TIP:** Remember how to set up a static route. You will make one of these entries for each route you wish to establish.

Default Routing

Default routing should be activated on each router so that if the router does not have a particular route in its routing table, the packet will not be discarded. Users on the network use something similar to this, called a default gateway. Default routes can only be used on stub networks, which have only one exit port out of the network. Default routes are set up with the same command used to set up static routes: **ip route**. *The only difference is that instead of using the network address and a subnet mask, you would use all 0s. The zeros are called wildcards.* An example of how to activate default routing is shown below.

After the wild cards, you list the address of the router interface you would like to set as the default route. The next command that must be used is **ip classless**. Cisco routers are "classful" by default, meaning that the routers need a default subnet mask on each router interface.

A default route will ensure that packets destined for remote addresses will not be dropped if there is no entry in the routing table. If you have version 12.x and up of the IOS, then IP classless is already turned on. **Before default routing can be used, static**

routes must be removed. The following commands are used to implement default routing:

Router>**en**
Router#**config t**
Router(config)#ip route 0.0.0.0 0.0.0.0   192.30.10.2
Router(config)#**ip classless**

EXAM TIP: The default route command also uses the "ip route" command followed by all 0s. The last address is the interface that you wish to use as the default route.

NOTE: The default route can also be referred to as a router or gateway of last resort.

Dynamic IP Routing

Dynamic IP routing is generally used on medium to large networks because manually maintaining a static routing table would be too much of a job for a networking staff. In dynamic IP routing, the routing tables are built and maintained by routing protocols.

Routed and Routing Protocols

Routed protocols are used between routers to deliver user data. Two good examples are IP and IPX. Routing protocols, on the other hand, only build and maintain routing tables. Examples of routing protocols are Routing Information Protocol (RIP) and Interior Gateway Routing Protocol (IGRP). Routing protocols only pass routing table information between routers.

Interior Routing Protocols: Interior routing protocols are connected to the Internet layer of the TCP/IP model. Below are examples of interior IP routing protocols:

- RIP: A distance-vector routing protocol
- IGRP: Cisco's proprietary distance-vector routing protocol
- OSPF: A link-state routing protocol
- Enhanced IGRP: Cisco's balanced distance-vector routing protocol

DISTANCE-VECTOR ROUTING PROTOCOLS

Distance-vector routing protocols can learn the distance and direction to all the network's connections (routes). But it listens to secondhand information when it gets routing table updates. RIP and IGRP are both distance-vector routing protocols. In RIP, the distance to the remote network is used to find the best path. Each router that a packet goes through is called a hop. RIP chooses to use the route with the fewest number of hops to a particular network. If there are multiple links with the same number of hop counts, RIP will use round-robin load balancing. It can do this for up to six equal cost links.

What does the routing protocol do?

- It dynamically builds the routing table with routes to all subnets in the network. Dynamic routes are the choice for administrators of large networks.

- It puts the best routes in the routing table, if there are multiple routes to a subnet. This allows your network to route data quicker.

- It recognizes when routes are no longer valid. These routes are then removed from the routing table, helping prevent routing loops.

- When routes are removed from the routing table and it finds another route to the remote network, it will add that route to the routing table.

- It can tell when routers are added to the network. It will dynamically place the best route to these new networks. It will also replace a lost route with the best currently available route. The amount of time it takes to replace a route is called convergence time.

The following are attributes of a router using RIP or IGRP distance-vector routing protocols:

- When you first enable RIP or IGRP on a router, directly connected subnets are already known and advertised.

- Neighboring routers learn route updates through broadcasts.

- Metrics are used to build a routing table. The lower the metric, the more trustworthy the route. In RIP the metric used is hops.

- Updates are provided by neighboring routers at specific intervals. If an update is not received when expected, the router will remove all the routes learned from that neighbor.

- Routes learned from a neighboring router are perceived to be through that router.

- Failed routes are advertised.

- When using distance-vector routing protocols, routing loops can occur because of bad routing information.

RIP and IGRP

Both RIP and IGRP collect routing information by major network number (this means these protocols collect network addresses, i.e., 192.10.3.0), a process called Classful Routing. IGRP is used in large networks, while RIP is used in small to moderate sized networks.

RIP and IGRP are both considered distance-vector routing protocols. Table 7-1 lists the characteristics of each:

Table 7-1: RIP and IGRP Characteristics

Feature	RIP (Defaults)	IGRP (Defaults)
*UPDATE TIMER	30 Seconds	90 Seconds
*METRIC	Hop Count	Function of Bandwidth and Delay
*HOLDDOWN TIMER	180	280

EXAM TIP: Learn the characteristics of distance-vector protocols. Also learn the defaults of RIP and IGRP in the chart above.

IGRP uses a metric that is better than RIP's system. The metric IGRP uses is bandwidth and delay to choose the better route. A longer hop route may be considered the better route if it is over faster links.

The metric used by IP RIP is hop count. As an update is received by a router the metric signifies the number of routers between the router receiving the update and each subnet. As a packet exits a router on its way to the remote network, the router will subtract one of the hop counts before sending it to the next router. When the counter reaches zero, the packet will be discarded.

If the router notices that a directly connected subnet has failed, it immediately sends another routing update on its other interfaces and does not wait for the routing update timer to expire.

If a link drops or goes off-line, routers must provide updates to the other routers in a network. The other routers use this information to update their routing tables. The amount of time it takes for this information to reach all parts of the network is called convergence time. Every time a change occurs on the network, it takes time for all the routers to update their tables. During convergence no data is allowed on the network.

Distance-vector routing protocols update every 30-90 seconds, depending on the protocol used. When each router receives an update, it then passes its entire routing table to all other known routers.

When distance-vector routers are first enabled, they receive information from their neighbors. They also learn the metrics (hops) to the other routers on each of their interfaces. A path is calculated using the number of hops (routers) from the sender to the receiver. The fewer the hops, the better.

The biggest problem with distance-vector routing protocols is routing loops. Routing loops happen when all of the routers on the network are not updated at the same time. The convergence time causes the data to loop around the network. This routing loop is called *counting to infinity*. A routing loop is caused by incorrect or secondhand information being provided to the routers.

Counting to infinity solutions are:

- *Triggered Updates* (sometimes called flash updates):
  - A new routing table is sent immediately in response to a topology change, which speeds up convergence.
  - Triggered updates do not wait for the update timer to expire.
  - Used with route poisoning to ensure that all routers know of failed routes before any hold-down timer can expire.

- **Maximum Hop Count:** The distance-vector protocol RIP allows a maximum hop count of 15. Any packet that needs 16 hops would be discarded. Actually what this means is that if a packet arrives at the 15th hop, it stays there and waits until its Time-to-Live expires and the package is discarded.

- **Split Horizon:** Enforces the rule that data cannot be sent back in the direction it came from. This reduces incorrect routing information, meaning that if data is received on one interface it cannot exit that same interface.

- **Split Horizon with Poison Reverse:** Usually just called Poison Reverse. Similar to Split Horizon, Poison Reverse will not advertise a route out the same interface that the route was learned.

- **Route Poisoning:** Used when a network goes down and an entry is made in the route table that the network is unreachable. If that network comes back up, the other routers on the network will be notified and their routing tables will be updated.

- **Hold-Downs:** Work with route poisoning to prevent regular update messages from reinstating a route that has just gone down. Hold-downs try to prevent routes from changing too rapidly by allowing time for either the downed route to come back up or the network to stabilize. This means that for a predetermined time frame any changes that affect a recently removed route are prevented. The length of time for the hold-down period is just greater than the period of time necessary to update the entire network with a routing change.

There are three occurrences that will reset the hold-down timer after a triggered update:

- When the hold-down timer expires.

- Another update is received indicating a network status change, like a new router is added.

- The router receives a processing task proportional to the number of lines in the internetwork.

EXAM TIP: I didn't highlight any of these areas because they are all important. Remember that the problem is "counting to infinity" and the solutions are: maximum hop count, split horizon, poison reverse, route poisoning, triggered updates, and hold-downs.

Configuring RIP Routing

The dynamic routing protocol RIP can be enabled using the following information:

- Log on to all local and remote routers.

- Enable RIP on the router with the **router rip command.**

- Tell RIP which network you wish to advertise, using the **network** command. Because RIP is dynamic, it is much easier to use than static routes, but uses the router's CPU for processing. RIP also takes up precious network bandwidth that is used when building and updating routing tables.

- Before you can use RIP, static and default routes must be removed with the **no ip route** command. If the static and defaults are not removed, you will not be able to communicate with remote routers. Static routes have an administrative distance of 1 and RIP's is 120. Because the static routes have a lower number, they will be used before RIP. When enabling RIP you need to know that RIP will only accept major networks. For example, if you enter an address like 192.30.20.40, the router will discard the host portion and use only the network portion of 192.30.20.0. Here are the steps to enable RIP:

  RouterA>**enable**
  RouterA#**config t**
  RouterA(config)#**router rip**
  RouterA(config-router)#**network 192.30.20.0**.
  RouterA(config-router)#**CTRL+Z**
  RouterA#**copy running startup**

EXAM TIP: You must know the "router rip" and "network" commands.
Note the level in which each step is performed. Look closely
at what the router prompt is before each command.

Monitoring RIP

Some tools that you can use to help monitor your RIP network include the following:

- *Show ip route:* Allows you to view the routing table. As you look at the routing table, the "R" is for RIP routes and the "C" is for directly connected networks. Also notice that the administrative distance for RIP is 120 and directly connected routes have a rating of 0. The administrative distance is used if two routing protocols advertise the same route to the same router. It will use the lowest administrative distance.

- *Show ip protocol:* Gives you information such as RIP timers, the network to which RIP is assigned, and routing information sources.

- *Show ip interface:* Type **show ip interface** s0, s1, or e0 to see Ethernet and serial ports individually.

- *Debug ip rip:* Turns on RIP debugging, giving you an update list that shows the routing updates as they are sent and received. Type **undebug ip rip** to stop debugging. Additionally the undebug all and no debug all commands can be used to turn off all debugging. To view all debugging that is currently enabled on the router, use the show debug command.

- *Debug ipx routing activity: This command will enable debugging for IPX RIP updates. This command is also used to show both source and destination addresses in ipx.*

- **Show ip route rip:** Allows you to see only the RIP-connected networks.

- **Show ip interface:** Shows a lot of statistics and how the interfaces are configured.

Removing RIP

If you are configuring a Cisco router and wish to remove RIP to install another routing protocol, use the **no router rip** command as shown:

RouterA#**config t**
RouterA(config)#**no router rip**
RouterA(config)#**CTRL+Z**
RouterA#**copy running startup**

Holding Down RIP Propagations

If you do not want RIP advertising your network to the Internet, use the **passive-interface** command. This command will stop RIP updates out that interface. Even though this command prevents RIP update broadcasts from being sent out, you can still receive inbound RIP updates.

RouterA#**config t**
RouterA(config)#**router rip**
RouterA(config-router)#**network 10.0.0.0**
Router(config-router)#passive-interface serial 0

EXAM TIP: Know the "passive-interface" command.

Link-State Protocols

When link-state protocols are enabled on a router, a database is built that acts like a map of the network. Routers using the link-state protocol know about all the routers in the network and how they interconnect. Link-state packets (LSPs) or "hello packets" are sent to inform other routers of distance links.

This link-state database is built by the shortest path first (SPF) algorithm. This algorithm is used to choose the best route and place it into the routing table. Avoiding loops and a quick convergence are the result of the database and the shortest path first algorithm.

The biggest concern with link-state is that it uses considerable processing power, memory, and bandwidth.

Link-State Compared to Distance-Vector

Distance-vector gets all its data from secondhand information, while link-state receives a complete and accurate view (database) of the network.

Distance-vector determines the best path by counting hops.
Link-state uses bandwidth analysis and other information to determine the best path.

Distance-vector reports topology changes in 30-second intervals by default. Link-state is triggered by topology changes, which result in faster convergence times.

Balanced Hybrid

Enhanced Interior Gateway Routing Protocol (**EIGRP**) uses the best attributes of distance-vector and link-state. EIGRP uses distance vectors with more accurate metric counts and can converge quickly with the use of link-state triggers. It uses a more efficient link-state protocol, which helps with the problem of high bandwidth, processor power, and memory needs.

> **EXAM TIP:** Link-state is no longer on the CCNA exam. It is now on the CCNP exam. Just read about it for real-world use. EIGRP is also not testable. But it could be put back into the CCNA exam. I believe in order to use the distance-vector protocol you need to compare it to link-state.

Interior Gateway Routing Protocol

Interior Gateway Routing Protocol (**IGRP**) is a Cisco proprietary distance-vector interior routing protocol used in larger autonomous systems. IGRP has a hop count of 255 (compared to RIP's 15) meaning that it can support up to 255 routers.

Administrative Distance

You have already learned that the administrative distance or metric is used to determine the trustworthiness of the routing update source. The lower the number, the more trusted the source. The most common methods include:

- Directly Connected Interface   0
- Static Route   1
- Internal Enhanced IGRP   90
- IGRP   100
- RIP   120

EXAM TIP: Learn the administrative distance for each of the most common commands shown above.

Configuring IGRP Routing

IGRP is configured in a manner similar to RIP. You use the **router IGRP** command and then identify the network number you want the router to advertise. *There is one major difference, however. You can have multiple IGRP routing protocols running between routers, so you have to enter the autonomous system number.*

An example of how to enable IGRP as the routing protocol for the autonomous system 20 is as follows:

```
Router>enable
RouterA#config t
*RouterA(config)#router igrp 20
*RouterA(config-router)#network 192.30.20.0
RouterA(config-router)#CTRL+Z
RouterA#copy running startup
```

Routes discovered by IGRP are identified by an "I" on the routing table.

Unlike RIP, IGRP uses delay, bandwidth, reliability, and load features when determining the routes. *Also, IGRP packets are sent out every 90 seconds by*

default, compared to 30 seconds for RIP. IGRP supports multiple paths (up to six unequal cost paths).

You can monitor IGRP and RIP with the same commands:

Show ip route
Show protocols
Show ip protocol
Show ip interfaces
Debug ip igrp
Trace

Again, IGRP must have an autonomous system number. All routers within an autonomous system must use the same number to communicate. An "autonomous system" is a set of routers under a common administration, and supports load balancing and load sharing.

EXAM TIP: Know how to enable IGRP on your router. First you use "router igrp" command followed by the autonomous system number. Then you use the "network" command followed by the network address. Remember what the router prompt reads at each level.

Open Shortest Path First

Open Shortest Path First (OSPF) is a link-state routing protocol. Each router has its own database of the topology. The advantages of OSPF include:

- OSPF allows you to assign up 65,535 metrics. If there is more than one route of equal cost, OSPF routers can balance the load of network traffic between all available and equally cost-effective routes.

- It sends broadcasts less often. Usually when a change is detected.

Enhanced Interior Gateway Routing Protocol

Enhanced Interior Gateway Routing Protocol (EIGRP) is a proprietary Cisco routing protocol that uses the advantages of link-state routing protocols and those of distance-vector protocols. It uses distance-vector features to determine the best paths, and link-state protocol features to route database updates.

EIGRP doesn't make periodic updates, but receives a complete routing table from its neighbors. After this initial communication, it sends only changes and only to the neighboring routers, thus improving bandwidth.

Exterior Routing Protocols

Exterior routing protocols were designed to communicate between autonomous systems (AS).

- **Exterior Gateway Protocol (EGP):** A dynamic routing protocol. EGP doesn't use metrics like interior routing protocols, so it can't detect or correct routing loops. EGP is a distance-vector protocol that allows ASs to communicate.

- **Border Gateway Protocol (BGP):** An inter-autonomous system protocol created for use on the Internet, which can determine routing loops.

Review Questions

1. Given a manual routing of IP route 172.16.10.0 255.255.255.0 172.16.40.1, which of the following are correct? (Select two.)
   a. 172.16.40.1 is the next hop.
   b. 172.16.10.0 is the network address.
   c. 255.255.255.0 is the next hop.
   d. 172.16.40.1 is the network address.

2. Routes that are directly connected will have an administrative distance of _____.
   a. 1
   b. 120
   c. 100
   d. 0

3. To set up a default route in a router you would use a subnet mask of _____.
   a. all 0s
   b. all 1s
   c. 255.255.255.255
   d. FF.FF.FF.FF

4. What techniques may be used to cure the routing loop problem?
    a. Counting to infinity
    b. Maximum hop count
    c. Split Horizon
    d. Route Poisoning
    e. Hold-Downs

5. What three occurrences will reset the hold-down timer after a triggered update?
    a. Hold-down timer expires.
    b. Another update is received indicating a network status change.
    c. The router receives a processing task proportional to the number of links in the internetwork.
    d. All the above

6. You are configuring a Local Area Network with RIP. The network is connected to the Internet, but you do not want to advertise your network. Which command stops the router from sending out any updates on the specified interface?
    a. #passive-interface serial 1
    b. >passive serial 1
    c. #serial 1 passive-interface
    d. >serial 1 passive-interface

7. Which two statements about IP RIP are true?
    a. It can handle an unlimited number of hops.
    b. It can handle 15 hops.
    c. It has an update timer default of 30 seconds.
    d. It has an update timer default of 90 seconds.

8. Which command sets IGRP as the routing protocol for autonomous system 100?
    a. router igrp 100
    b. network 100
    c. router igrp
    d. network igrp

9. What are two types of routing?
   a. Static
   b. Dynamic
   c. Manual
   d. Automatic

10. How is RIP enabled on a router?
    a. Router#router rip
    b. Router(config-if)route rip
    c. Router>router rip
    d. Router (config)#router rip

11. Which of the following are considered exterior routing protocols? (Select all that apply.)
    a. EGP
    b. RIP
    c. BGP
    d. IGRP

12. Which of the following are attributes of IGRP? (Select four.)
    a. Update timer default of 90 seconds
    b. Update timer default of 30 seconds
    c. Uses hop counts
    d. Uses bandwidth and delay
    e. Hold-down timer default of 180
    f. Hold-down timer default of 280

Answers and Explanations

1. **a, b.** The first number is the destination network address of 172.16.10.0 and the next number is the subnet mask (255.255.255.0). 172.16.40.1 is the IP address of the next hop router. For a good example see page 147.

2. **d.** Directly connected routes are most trustworthy and have an administrative distance of 0.

3. **a.** Default routes are set up with the same command used to set up static routes. The only difference is that instead of using the network address and a subnet mask, you would use all 0s.

4. **b, c, d, e.** The techniques used to cure the routing loop problem are maximum hop count, split horizon, split horizon with poison reverse, route poisoning, triggered updates, and hold-downs. Remember counting to infinity is the problem and the other answers are the solutions.

5. **d.** There are three occurrences that will reset the hold-down timer after a triggered update: When the hold-down timer expires, another update is received indicating a network status change, like a new router is added, and the router receives a processing task proportional to the number of lines in the internetwork.

6. **a.** If you do not want RIP advertising your network to the Internet, use the passive-interface command. This command will stop RIP updates out that interface. Even though this command prevents RIP update broadcasts from being sent out, you can still receive inbound RIP updates.

7. **b, c.** IP RIP has a hop count of 15, meaning that it can support up to 15 routers, and sends out packets every 30 seconds by default.

8. **a.** You use the router IGRP command and then identify the network number you want the router to advertise. You can have multiple IGRP routing protocols running between routers, so you have to enter the autonomous system number.

9. **a, b.** There are three ways that a routing table can be built, which are static, default, and dynamic routing.

10. **d.** RIP is enabled on a router by using the router rip command.

11. **a, c.** EGP and BGP are exterior routing protocols. RIP and IGRP are interior IP routing protocols.

12. **a, c, d, f.** The metric IGRP uses bandwidth and delay to choose the better route and sends packets out every 90 seconds with the hold-down timer default of 280. IGRP has a hop count of 255, meaning that it can support up to 255 routers.

Chapter

Configuring IPX

These are the areas that are generally testable on the CCNA examination:

IPX addressing and routing:

- Describe the two parts of network addressing and then identify the parts in specific protocol address examples.
- List the required IPX address and encapsulation type.

Introduction

This chapter has many testable areas.

You will first learn the structure of an IPX address, which is made up of 80 bits: 32 bits for the networking address and 48 bits for the host address. The network portion is determined by the network administrator, while the host portion, the machine's MAC address, is automatically assigned.

Next, you will learn the different types of data-link encapsulation that IPX can use on the network, and how to enable them.

You will also learn the Novell RIP defaults as compared to IP RIP, and that IPX RIP uses ticks and hops. (A tick is 1/18 of one second.)

We will then cover how to enable IPX routing on a router. This is done at the global level with the **ipx routing** command, and then enabled with the **ipx network** command followed by the network number.

Finally, you will learn how to set up secondary addresses using the **ipx network** command, and how to set up subinterfaces using the **int e0.30** command.

NOVELL IPX PROTOCOL STACK

Novell IPX (Internetwork Packet Exchange) has been in use since the 1980s, and there are still many Novell networks worldwide. Novell's latest product, NetWare 5, has TCP/IP as its default protocol, but it still provides support for IPX.

IPX has an 80-bit address structure; a 32-bit network part and a 48-bit *host (MAC address)* part.

> **EXAM TIP: This should be easy to remember. IPX is made up of 80 bits with 32 bits as the network portion and 48 bits as the host portion. Finally, know that the host portion is usually the NIC's MAC address.**

Data-link encapsulation, of course, occurs in the Data Link layer of the OSI model. Before a frame exits a router, data-link encapsulation determines the details of data-link headers and trailers that will be placed around a packet. One problem with IPX is that you can use many different types of encapsulation, sometimes at the same time. This can cause problems in today's networks because every device on the network must use the same type of encapsulation to communicate. Table 8-1 lists the IPX Ethernet encapsulations paired up with what Cisco calls them:

Table 8-1: IPX Ethernet Encapsulations

Novell Name	Cisco IOS
Ethernet_II	ARPA
Ethernet_802.3	Novell-Ether
Ethernet_802.2	SAP
Ethernet_Snap	SNAP
Fddi_Snap	SNAP
Token-Ring_Snap	SNAP
Fddi-raw	Novell_fddi

EXAM TIP: Learn the above table forward and backward. Notice that the Novell types with "snap" after them are called SNAP by Cisco. Those are three "freebies," so you only have to memorize the other four.

If you have a Novell network with more than one encapsulation type on it, every router will have to be configured to process each type. Or better yet, you can just convert the network to use only one encapsulation type.

Another good reason to have only one type of encapsulation on your network is that it makes the network easier to troubleshoot. This is because clients or servers using different encapsulation types cannot communicate directly, so a router must do this for them.

RIP for IPX works almost the same as IP RIP. The biggest difference is that IPX advertises IPX network numbers instead of IP subnet numbers.

RIP for IPX is compared to RIP for IP in Table 8-2:

Table 8-2: RIP for IPX vs. RIP for IP

Novell RIP	IP RIP
*Uses 60-second update timer (default)	Uses 30-second update timer (default)
*Uses timer ticks (primary metric) and hop count as secondary	Uses hop count as only metric

*IPX RIP uses ticks and hops, a tick being 1/18 of one second. This metric tracks the number of ticks it takes for a packet to reach its end destination. LANs have a default of one tick and WANs have a default of six ticks. If the number of ticks is the same for two routes, the number of hops will be used to determine the best route. The tick metric is more efficient than hops and, when used in combination, makes IPX RIP perform better. The time it takes for a packet to reach its destination is more important than the number of hops.

EXAM TIP: Learn the Novell RIP defaults as compared to IP RIP. Also, know that IPX RIP uses ticks and hops, a tick being 1/18 of one second.

SERVICE ADVERTISEMENT PROTOCOL

Service Advertisement Protocol (SAP) is used by its servers to advertise the services it provides to its network clients. SAP is an important aspect of the IPX protocol, but SAP can be challenging as you try to scale your IPX network.

SAP utilizes a feature similar to the distance-vector routing protocol's split-horizon to stop devices from advertising SAP information learned on an interface and then sending it out the same interface. SAP information is placed in a SAP table on the server or router. IPX SAP disseminates service information to all the servers and routers, ensuring that the same information is placed on each device.

SAP information is important because when a client comes online on the network, it sends a Get Nearest Server (GNS) message to find the server. The overall goal of the client is to log in to its preferred server, which will then allow the client to use its full SAP table and show the IPX address of the preferred server.

IPX Addressing

IPX addresses use 80 bits (10 bytes) for addressing purposes. IPX, like IP, has a network and node portion. *The first four bytes represent the network address, and the last six bytes represent the node or host address.* IPX does not use network classes, so the network and host portions remain constantly the same length.

IPX network numbers are assigned by the administrator and must be unique throughout the network. Unlike IP, the node portion is assigned automatically. *In most cases, the MAC address of the machine is used as the node portion of the address.*

The benefits and characteristics of IPX are:

- No need to manually configure each host, saving a lot of time for busy administrators.

- No need for the ARP protocol, because the hardware address is part of the IPX host portion.

- The network portion of the IPX address is the first eight hex digits (example: 0000004b) and the remaining 12 hex digits (example: 0000.7614.44C9) are the host portion. Here is how it looks together: *4b.0000.7614.44C9*.

NOTE: When referring to the network the leading 0s are usually dropped.

> **EXAM TIP: Know that the first four bytes represent the network address and the last six bytes represent the host portion. Also, know that the host portion is the NIC's MAC address. Finally, be able to select an IPX address from a list of other protocol addresses.**

Enabling IPX Routers

There are two steps to perform when enabling IPX on a router. The first is to globally enable IPX on the router with the **ipx routing** command. Then, each interface must be activated with the **ipx network** command followed by a network number. Here is what the two steps look like:

> RouterA#**config t**
> **RouterA(config)#ipx routing   (Global)*
> RouterA(config)**CTRL+Z**

NOTE: When IPX routing is enabled, IPX RIP is automatically enabled. This means you do not need to use a separate command to enable IPX RIP.

> RouterA(config)#**interface s0**
> **RouterA(config-if)#ipx network 10   (Interface level)*
> RouterA(config-if)#**CTRL+Z**

NOTE: This is how you enable IPX on an interface with a network address of 10.

> **EXAM TIP: Know how to enable IPX routing on a router. It is done at the global level with the "ipx routing" command. Then the individual interface must be enabled with the "ipx network" command followed by the network number.**

Monitoring IPX on Cisco Routers

- ***Show IPX Route:** *Allows you to view the IPX routing table.*

  RouterA#**show ipx route**

- ***IPX maximum-paths:** The Cisco IOS does not support parallel paths between routers by default. You need to use the command ***ipx maximum-paths 2** (default is 2 and maximum is 512). This allows the router to provide load balancing by using multiple paths. This is sometimes called round-robin load balancing.

- ***Show IPX Traffic:** Provides the number and type of IPX packets received and transmitted by the router.

  RouterA#**show ipx traffic**

- ***Show IPX Interface e0:** Shows individual interface settings, such as the IPX address of each interface.

  RouterA#**show ipx interface e0**

- **Show IPX Servers:** Displays the contents of the SAP table on a router.

  RouterA#**show ipx servers**

- **Show Protocols**: Shows the IP address and encapsulation type of each interface.

  RouterA#**show protocols**

EXAM TIP: Know that "show ipx route" will allow you to view the IPX routing table. The "ipx maximum-paths" command allows the router to support parallel paths. The "show ipx traffic" command will provide the number and type of IPX packets received and transmitted by the router. Finally, "show ipx interface" will show you the individual interface settings.

Adding Secondary Addresses

Remember that an IPX network can use different encapsulation types. If you want to configure the router to use multiple frame types, you can either use the secondary command or create a subinterface. If you don't use the encapsulation command, the default frame type Novell-Ether (802.3) is used. The commands you can use to configure multiple encapsulation types on your network are as follows:

- ***Secondary Addresses:*** To configure a secondary address you use the **ipx network** command. This is followed by the network number, the word encap, and then the encapsulation type. Notice the last command in the following example. Sec means secondary, and without this you will replace an entry already on the router.

    RouterA#**config t**
    RouterA(config)#**int e0**
    RouterA(config-if)#**ipx network 14a encap sap sec**

NOTE: As you configure secondary addresses, each frame type needs a different IPX network number to operate correctly.

- ***Subinterfaces: Creating subinterfaces allows one physical interface to support multiple logical IPX networks.*** Again, each subinterface must have a unique IPX network number and a unique encapsulation type. To set up subinterfaces, use the **interface ethernet port number** command.

    RouterA(config)#**int e0.30**   (means interface ethernet port number)
    RouterA(config-subif)#**ipx network 30a encap sap**
    RouterA(config-subif)#**CTRL+Z**

EXAM TIP: You must know how to set up secondary addresses using the "ipx network" command. More than likely you will need to know how to set up subinterfaces using the "int e0.30" command.

1. Which of the following have correctly matched the Novell frame type to the Cisco encapsulation type? (Select all that apply.)
   a. Ethernet_802.3   Novell-Ether
   b. Ethernet 802.2   SAP
   c. Ethernet_II   ARPA
   d. Fddi_Snap   SNAP
   e. Token-Ring_Snap   SNAP
   f. Fddi-raw   Novell-fddi
   g. All the above

2. Which of the following is a valid IPX address?
   a. 4a.0000.0c00.23fe
   b. 172.16.10.20
   c. 127.0.0.1
   d. FF.FF.FF.FF

3. You are working on an IPX-enabled network. Which of the following commands will allow the router to accept the possibility that there might be more than one path to the same destination?
   a. maximum-paths
   b. ipx maximum-paths
   c. enable ipx maximum-paths
   d. set maximum-paths

4. You are working on an IPX-enabled network. Which command would you use to see a summary of the number and type of IPX packets that a router has received and transmitted?
   a. view ipx traffic
   b. sh traffic ipx
   c. sh ipx traffic
   d. sh ipx packets

5. Which of the following commands will show you the IPX address of an interface? (Select all that apply.)
   a. show protocols
   b. show ipx interface
   c. show ipx address
   d. show interface ipx

6. What command has the proper syntax to specify a subinterface #4?
   a. subinterface s0.4
   b. ip interface s0.4
   c. set interface s0.4
   d. interface s0.4

7. What does IPX RIP use to make routing decisions?
   a. Ticks and hops
   b. Ticks only
   c. Hops only
   d. Bandwidth and delay

8. Which of the following commands will allow you to view an IPX routing table?
   a. show route ipx
   b. show ipx route
   c. view ipx route
   d. show ipx int

9. Which of the following commands will enable IPX routing on a router? (Select two.)
   a. router rip
   b. ipx routing
   c. network ipx
   d. ipx network

10. Which of the following best describes the host portion of an IPX address? (Select two.)
    a. It is usually the MAC address.
    b. It is usually the network address.
    c. It is made up of 48 bits.
    d. It is made up of 32 bits.

1. **g.** The IPX Ethernet encapsulations paired up with what Cisco calls them are shown in Table 8-1. Review this table and memorize it.

2. **a.** 172.16.10.20 is a Class B IP address, with 127 reserved for the Ping command in the IP address. FF.FF.FF.FF is used as a broadcast address in the IP protocol. The network portion of the IPX address 4a.0000.0c00.23fe is 4a and the host portion (which is the MAC address) is 0000.0c00.23fe.

3. **b.** The Cisco IOS does not support parallel paths between routers by default. You need to use the command *ipx maximum-paths 2* (default is 2 and maximum is 512). This allows the router to provide load balancing by using multiple paths. This is sometimes called round-robin load balancing.

4. **c.** *show ipx traffic* provides the number and type of IPX packets received and transmitted by the router. IOS can understand abbreviations, such as *sho* or *sh*. This is true of most of the IOS commands. On version 10.3 and earlier, however, you have to write the full command.

5. **a, b.** *show ipx interface e0* shows individual interface settings, such as the IPX address of each interface.

6. **d.** The proper syntax to set up subinterfaces is: *int interfaceID.subinterfaceID* or *interface interfaceID.subinterfaceID*.

7. **a.** IPX RIP uses ticks and hops to make routing decisions. It tracks the number of ticks it takes for a packet to reach its end destination. If the number of ticks is the same for two routes, the number of hops will be used to determine the best route.

8. **b.** *show ipx route* allows you to view the IPX routing table.

9. **b, d.** *ipx routing* will globally enable IPX on the router. After that, each interface must be activated with the *ipx network* command.

10. **a, c.** IPX is made up of 80 bits with 32 bits as the network portion and 48 bits as the host portion. The last six bytes of an IPX address represent the host address, which is usually the NIC's MAC address.

Chapter 9

Access Lists

These are the areas that are generally testable on the CCNA examination:

Filtering IP traffic:

- Configure standard and extended access lists to filter IP traffic.
- Monitor and verify selected access list operations on the router.

In this chapter you will learn to read an access list and understand what actions will be performed. Be aware of the implied "deny" at the end of the access list.

You'll learn how to create an access list with the **access-list** command and how to apply it to the interface with the **ip access-group** command. Also, you will learn that the **show ip interface** and **show running-config** commands are used to view an access list.

On the exam you can expect to see two or three questions that give you an access list and ask you to determine what action will take place. I recommend that you memorize the format for each type of access list. You must also know that the number range for extended IP access lists is 100-199.

ACCESS LISTS OVERVIEW

Access lists are similar to packet filtering on an NT server. They are lists of conditions set by the administrator to control access to a particular network segment, by limiting access to a specific router's interface, and for optimizing the network traffic. Access lists can be used to control inbound or outbound traffic on the interface. It's important to understand that the direction (inbound or outbound) is relative to the router's interface. For example, if the server is connected to one of the router's interfaces, the packet addressed to that server is outbound traffic for the router's interface.

Once the access list is applied to the interface, all packets are analyzed and compared with entries in the access list. If one of the conditions in the access list matches the packet's information (IP address, network address, port number, protocol type, etc.), the router acts according to instructions in that access list. The packet is compared with each line in the access list, one at a time. Once the packet matches the condition on one of the lines in the access list, the router acts upon that condition and no further comparisons take place. If the packet does not match any of the conditions on the access list, the packet is discarded just as if the list contained a **deny any** entry. This is important to remember when creating the access list.

There are two types of access lists: **standard** and **extended**. Standard access lists can analyze the packet based on the source IP address. A packet's source IP address can be used to either allow or deny access (either inbound or outbound) to the interface.

Extended access lists can, in addition to source IP address, also include entries for:

- Destination IP address
- Port number
- Protocol type

A router can have many different access lists, but only one access list is allowed per interface. Each access list must have a unique number. This number must be within a specific range, depending on the type of access list. There are two steps in configuring an access list (either standard or extended):

1. Create the access list in Global Configuration mode.
2. Apply the access list to the interface in Interface Configuration mode.

Access list details:

- They filter traffic to and from your network, controlling access with certain conditions. This provides security for your network.
- They are used to filter packets on routers. Security can be assured by this process.

Filtering attributes:

- In order for filtering to work, packets must originate outside the router.
- Filtering can take place when packets enter an interface.
- Filtering can also take place before packets exit an interface.
- The term "deny" is used to tell the router that the packet will be filtered.
- The term "permit" is used to tell the router that the packet will not be filtered.
- There is an implied "deny all traffic" at the end of each access list. This means that if the packet does not meet the criteria in an access list, the packet will not be granted access.

Access list processing steps:

- As the packet enters the router, it is matched against the first statement in the access list.

- If a match is made in the first line entry of the access list, it performs the action (i.e., permit or deny).

- If a match is not made in the first statement of the access list, the packet will then be matched against the next entry, and so on.

- If none of the entries in the access matches the packet, the implied "deny any" will be performed. Because of this, an access list must have one "permit" statement.

EXAM TIP: Fully understand the access list process.

Standard IP Access Lists

Standard access lists can only filter based on the source address in the packet's IP header. The filtering process is not concerned with a subnet mask, only the IP address. The fields used in a standard IP access list include:

Access-list (number)   (permit or deny)   (source address)
      1   2   3

1. This is the access list number, which depends on the type of access list.

2. Here you will use the term permit or deny.

3. This is the source address.

Standard access lists are very simple to configure, but they can only filter the traffic based on the source address. If you want to filter the traffic based on the source and destination address, as well as port number, you need to use extended access lists.

NOTE: IP standard access lists are given numbers between 1 and 99.

Here is what a typical access list entry looks like:

RouterA#**config t**
RouterA(config)#**access-list 11 permit 192.40.20.2**

Even though the access list has been configured, it won't start filtering until it is applied to an interface.

    RouterA#**config t**
    RouterA(config)#**interface e0**
    RouterA(config-if)#**ip access-group 11 out**
    RouterA(config-if)#**CTRL+Z**

NOTE: The 11 in the third line refers to access list number 11. The out informs the router to use the access list on outbound packets, not inbound packets. "Out" means packets leaving the router's interface and going out to the network. "In" means packets arriving at the router's interface from the network. After the access list is created, you must apply it to an interface with an inbound or outbound list. *It is important to note that the access-group command is defined at the interface level.* It is equally important to understand that if you use the access-group command on an interface and there is no access list created, you will receive an error message.

> **EXAM TIP:** Be able to read an access list and understand what action will be performed. Be aware of the implied "deny" at the end of the access list. After you create the access list with the "access-list" command, you need to apply it to an interface with the "ip access-group" command.

Creating Access Lists

- You can have only one access list per interface, per protocol, or per direction. This means you can have only one outbound or inbound access list per interface.

- When you create a new entry in an access list, it will be placed at the bottom of the list. Be sure to review the access list's top entries because they may make a match, thereby eliminating the purpose of the new entry.

- You cannot remove a single entry from an access list. If you try to do so, the entire list will be removed. Your best option is to copy the list and edit it with a text editor.

- Remember, after you create an access list, you must apply it to an interface or filtering will not occur.

- Place IP standard access lists as close to the destination as possible.

- Place IP extended access lists as close to the source as possible.

Wildcard Masking

Wildcards are used to specify a specific host or subnet. Wildcards allow you to grant one workstation access, but deny access to the rest of the segment.

To block access to an entire subnet, use the network ID followed by 255. An example of an access list using wildcards:

RouterA(config)#**access-list 11 permit 192.40.30.2   0.0.0.0**
RouterA(config)#**access-list 10 permit 192.40.30.3   0.0.0.255**
RouterA(config)#**interface e0**
RouterA(config-if)#**ip access-group 11 out**
RouterA(config-if)#**CTRL+Z**

NOTE: Using a wildcard mask 0.0.0.0 means that the IP must match up exactly. Using 0.0.0.255 only requires that the first three numbers match exactly, and the last number can be any number. Keep in mind that you can use only "0" or "255". Later on you will learn the host command.

Two commands to view access lists:

- *Show ip interface: Shows which interfaces have access lists set.* For example, if you view the IP access list on the serial 0 interface, use the **show ip interface s0** command.

- *Show running-config: Shows the access lists and which interfaces have access lists set.*

NOTE: When configuring an access list to be applied to only one host, use 0.0.0.0 after the IP address or use the word "host". They both mean the same thing and would be used as follows:

172.12.30.55 0.0.0.0

host 172.12.30.55

EXAM TIP: Know how to create an access list and how to apply it to the interface with the "ip access-group" command. Also, know that the "show ip interface" and "show running-config" commands are used to view access lists.

Extended IP Access Lists

Extended IP access lists are similar to standard IP access lists. Extended lists are used for packets entering or exiting an interface, and can filter based on the following:

Source Address/Destination Address/IP protocol (TCP, UDP)/Port information (i.e. 80, 25)

Access-list (number) (permit or deny) (protocol) (source) (destination) (port)
           1   2   3   4   5   6

1. The number of the access list. *The access list number range for extended IP access lists is 100-199.*

2. The action you want to take: permit or deny.

3. The protocol you will use to take action on (i.e., TCP, UDP)

4. The source IP address.

5. The destination IP address

6. The port number you want to filter

Here is an example of what an extended IP access list would look like:

```
RouterA#config t
RouterA(config)#access-list 101 permit tcp host 192.40.30.2 any tcp eq 23
RouterA(config)#interface e0
RouterA(config-if)#ip access-group 101 out
RouterA(config-if)#CTRL+Z
```

NOTE: This access list will permit TCP traffic on port 23 (telnet) from IP address 192.40.30.2 to any IP address. Instead of using a port number, you can use the name of the TCP protocol, such as telnet, dns, echo, ftp, etc.

EXAM TIP: On the exam you can expect to see two or three questions that give you an access list and ask what action will take place. I recommend that you memorize the format for each type of access list. Also know that the number range for extended IP access lists is 100-199.

Access list examples:

- From the Configuration mode, type access-list [number] [permit or deny] [source address]. For example,

    access-list 10 deny 222.122.122.100

    will create an access list number 10 with the condition to deny packets with the source address of 222.122.122.100. It's important to remember that all access lists have implicit deny at the last line. So, when we created our access list 10, it looks like this:

    deny 222.122.122.100
    deny any

    This means that all traffic will be denied. This is not what we wanted to achieve. To correct this problem and deny only packets with source address 222.122.122.100, we need to add another line to our access list. Type **access-list 10 permit any** and our access list now looks like this:

    deny 222.122.122.100
    permit any
    deny any

NOTE: 0.0.0.0 and 255.255.255.255 are different wild cards and are used in combination with each other. The term "any" is the same as using the wildcards 0.0.0.0 255.255.255.255. The two singular wildcards together are called the plural of wildcard masking.

The last line **deny any** will always be there because it is inserted automatically by the router, but it will never be used because once the condition is met (either **deny 222.122.122.100** or **allow any**), the router does not read any further lines in the access list.

When creating an access list with a **deny** directive, it's important to add another line that allows all or some traffic, or you will just shut down the router.

- When creating an access list that includes an entire network or subnet, you should use wildcard masking. A wildcard mask is somewhat similar to the subnet mask. Here is an example:

    access-list 12 permit 222.122.122.0 0.0.0.255

    In this example we created an access list that permits traffic from all hosts on a network 222.122.122.0. The wildcard mask of 0.0.0.255 tells the router that the first 3 octets must match up exactly, and the last octet is any number from 0 to 255.

- You can have many access lists on a router, but they don't do anything until you apply a list to an interface. To do so, you must first enter an Interface Configuration mode. For example, from the config mode, type **int e0**. The router prompt will change to Router(config-if)#, indicating that all the changes made here will only be applied to an interface e0. To apply an access list, type: **Router(config-if)#ip access-group 10 [in or out]**. For example, to apply an access list 10 to control outbound traffic, type **ip access-group 10 out**. To deactivate an access list type **no ip access list 10 out**. On a router with only 2 interfaces, one serial and one Ethernet, applying an access list for inbound traffic to the serial interface produces the same effect as applying the same access list to the Ethernet interface for outbound traffic. For multiport routers you have to decide whether to apply an access list to inbound or outbound traffic based on the needs of the network.

These are the areas that are generally testable on the CCNA examination:

Filtering IPX traffic and SAPs:

- Configure IPX access lists and SAP filters to control basic Novell traffic.

- Monitor and verify selected access list operations on the router.

IPX access lists are used to filter packets sent by clients and servers. They can also be used to filter SAP updates sent by servers and routers. SAP filters are commonly used to prevent clients and servers from trying to send packets. *These access lists have a range of 1000-1099.*

The IPX filtering overview:

- The packet is matched against the first access-list statement.

- When a match is made, the action defined in this access-list statement (permit or deny) is performed. The packet does not look at other entries after a match is made.

- If a match is not made in the first access list entry, the packet is matched to the second entry, then the next entry, and so on.

- If the packet cannot be matched with any entry, the deny action is performed.

Standard IPX access lists:

- Standard access lists for IPX can check the source and destination network number. They can also check the node part of the source and destination addresses and use a wildcard mask to only examine parts of the node part of the addresses.

Extended IPX access lists:

- Extended access lists for IPX can check the following additional items when comparing a packet to an access-list command:
  - The source and destination socket
  - The protocol type: NCP, RIP, SAP, SPX, NetBIOS, or "any"
  - A wildcard mask to match multiple networks with one statement

SAP access lists:

- SAP filtering provides two functions: filtering the services listed in outgoing SAP updates, and filtering services listed in received SAP updates. The first function reduces the information sent to the router's neighboring IPX servers and routers. The second function limits what a router adds to its SAP table. And unlike packet filters, SAP filters examine the data inside the packet.

- Two main reasons exist for using SAP filters: First, SAP updates can consume a large amount of bandwidth. If a user in one division never needs services from servers in another division, there is no need to waste bandwidth advertising the services. Secondly, SAP filters can accomplish the same task as most IPX packet filters, but with less overhead.

Standard IPX Access Lists

Most of what you have learned about IP access lists still applies here, but there are some important changes. Standard IPX access lists allow or deny packets based on source and destination IPX addresses. Standard IP access lists use only source addresses.

Access-list (number) (permit/deny) (source) (destination)

RouterA#**config t**
RouterA(config)#**access-list 801 permit 10 20**
RouterA(config)#**access-list 802 deny 30 10**
RouterA(config)#**interface e0**
RouterA(config-if)#**ipx access-group 801 out**
RouterA(config-if)#**ipx access-group 802 out**
RouterA(config-if)#**CTRL+Z**

Apply Access Lists

Just like in IP access lists, there is an **implicit deny** at the end of an IPX access list. To apply an IPX access list, go to **Interface Configuration mode** and type:

Router(config-if)#**ipx access-group [number] [in or out]**

For example: Router(config-if)#***ipx access-group 801 in***

Examples:

Just like IP access lists, IPX access lists are created from the Global Configuration mode.

access-list 801 permit 40 80

This access list will permit IPX traffic from network 40 to network 80. We use number 801 because IPX access list numbers must be between 800-899.

To define any network in IPX access lists you use -1 (minus one).

access-list 805 deny -1 -1 will deny IPX traffic from any network to any network.

NOTE: *The range for standard IPX access lists is 800-899. It is important to know that when the −1 network address is used it means any IPX network address.* This is the same as the "**any**" keyword used in IP access lists.

EXAM TIP: Know that the range for standard IPX access lists is 800-899. It is important to know that when the −1 network address is used it means any IPX network address. Learn the format for this type of access list.

The commands used to view an IPX access list include:

- sh ipx e0
- sh ipx ether0
- sh ipx int ether0

NOTE: The commands are the same but abbreviated differently.

Extended IPX Access Lists

Extended IPX access lists filter based on the following:

Source network/node
Destination network/node
IPX protocol (SAP, special)
IPX socket

The syntax for creating an extended IPX access list is:

access-list [number] [permit/deny] [protocol] [source] [socket] [destination] [socket]

NOTE: *The range for these lists is 900-999.*

EXAM TIP: Usually, you only need to know standard and extended IP access lists, but don't leave anything to chance. Know what each portion of all the access lists means. Know that the range is 900-999. Be careful on the exam, as some answers may use the wrong access list number. Select the answer with the correct number range.

Monitoring Access Lists

There are several commands that you can use to view your access lists from Privileged mode:

- *Show access-list* will display all access lists configured on the router, access list numbers, and all the lines in them. *If you want to view a specific access list, use the command show access-list (number).*

- *Show ip interface* (or sh ip int) will display IP interface configurations, including numbers of outgoing and inbound access lists.

- *Show ipx interface* will show interfaces that are configured with IPX protocols, and IPX access lists associated with them.

- *Show running-configuration*, entered from the Privileged mode, will show running configuration, and access groups applied to particular interfaces.

- *Show access* will list the entire access list on a router. It does not show which interface the list is set on.

EXAM TIP: Be certain to learn the commands you can use to view your access lists from Privileged mode:

Access Lists

Table 9-1 shows access-list ranges.

Table 9-1: Access-List Ranges

Range	Access List
*1-99	IP Standard Access List
*100-199	IP Extended Access List
200-299	Protocol Type-code Access List
300-399	DECnet Access List
*600-699	AppleTalk Access List
700-799	48-bit MAC Address Access List
*800-899	IPX Standard Access List
*900-999	IPX Extended Access List
*1000-1099	IPX SAP Access List
1100-1199	Extended 48-bit MAC Address Access List
1200-1299	IPX Summary Address Access List

Access List Characteristics

Table 9-2 shows the access list characteristics.

Table 9-2: Access List Characteristics

Access List	Filters	Wildcard Masks	Additional Notes
Standard IP	Source IP address field in the packet's IP header	When the IP is broken down to binary, the 1s allow everything and the 0s must match exactly	Wildcard mask examples: 0.0.0.0=entire address must match. 0.255.255.255=only the first octet must match, the rest will allow everything. 255.255.255.255=allow everything
Extended IP	Source IP or Destination IP, or TCP or UDP Source or Destination Ports, or Protocol	Same as standard	The key word ANY implies any IP value is allowed, the keyword HOST implies the IP has to match exactly
Standard IPX	Packets sent by clients and servers, and SAP updates sent by servers and routers	Configured as a hexadecimal number instead of binary	-1 means any and all network numbers; works as "ANY"
Extended IPX	Source Network or Node, or Destination Network or Node, or IPX Protocol, or IPX Socket, or SAP	Match multiple networks with one statement, again in hexadecimal	The most practical use of the protocol type is for NetBIOS
SAP	Sent and received SAP traffic	N/A	Updates its own SAP tables. Again uses -1 to mean "ANY"

NOTE: At the end of every access list is an unwritten, yet implied deny any or deny all. The order of the list is very important...watch for order on the exam. Read access list questions, particularly the filtering criteria, thoroughly before selecting an answer!

1. What three commands can be used to view an IPX Ethernet access list?
   a. sh ipx e0
   b. sh ipx ether0
   c. sh ipx int ether0
   d. All the above

2. You are configuring access lists for Cisco routers. There is an implicit "deny any" at the end of each access list that discards packets that don't match up to any lines in the access list. (T/F)
   a. True
   b. False

3. There is an implicit "deny any" at the end of each access list that discards packets that don't match up to any lines in the access list. The access list must contain one PERMIT statement. (T/F)
   a. True
   b. False

4. Every access list must have at least one permit statement, otherwise the implicit deny will shut down all traffic. (T/F)
   a. True
   b. False

5. When a router is examining a packet to pass it through an access list, it considers each line of the access list, starting at the top and proceeding to the bottom. (T/F)
   a. True
   b. False

6. If a packet does not match any of the lines in the access list, it is _____.
   a. processed against another access list
   b. discarded
   c. placed into buffers
   d. sent to a DNS Server

7. If a packet is not explicitly allowed by an access list, it is _____.
   a. processed against another access list
   b. placed into buffers
   c. discarded
   d. sent to a DNS server

8. Which of the following items that extended IP access lists use for filtering is also used by standard IP access lists?
   a. Source address
   b. Destination address
   c. IP protocol
   d. Port information

9. The standard IP access list uses which of the following number ranges?
   a. 100-199
   b. 1000-1099
   c. 800-899
   d. 1-99

10. Access lists are created in which of the following router modes?
   a. Global Configuration mode
   b. User mode
   c. Interface Configuration mode
   d. Subinterface Configuration mode

11. The line "RouterA(config) #access-list 1 deny 10.10.10.0 0.0.0.255" will _____, when configuring an access list on router A.
   a. allow all packets from network 10.10.10.0
   b. allow all packets from network 0.0.0.255
   c. block all packets from network 10.10.10.0
   d. block all packets from network 0.0.0.25

12. The access-group command is defined at which of the following levels?
   a. Global level
   b. Subinterface level
   c. User level
   d. Interface level

Access Lists

13. Which of the following steps is used to configure a standard access list?
   a. Configure the access list in Global Configuration mode.
   b. Apply the access list to an interface in Interface Configuration mode.
   c. Configure the access list in Interface Configuration mode.
   d. Apply the access list to an interface in Global Configuration mode.

14. When applying an access list to an interface, the rule is that only one list per protocol is allowed inbound and only one list per protocol is allowed outbound. (T/F)
   a. True
   b. False

15. Which of the following are correct ways for referring only to host 172.12.30.55 in an access list? (Select two.)
   a. 172.12.30.55 0.0.0.0
   b. 172.12.30.55 255.255.255.255
   c. host 172.12.30.55
   d. host 0.0.0.0

16. What commands can be used to view the access list for an interface? (Select two.)
   a. show ip access list
   b. show access-list
   c. show ip interface
   d. show running-config

17. Which command is used to view the IP access list on the serial0 interface?
   a. show ip interface s0
   b. show access-list
   c. show interface s0 ip
   d. show ip s0 interface

18. What is the correct Cisco IOS command for monitoring an IP access list on the router, but does not show which interface the list is set on?
   a. show ip interface
   b. show access-list
   c. show interface ip
   d. show access-list interface

19. What IOS command will list the entire access list running on a router, but does not show which interface the list is set on?
    a. show access-1
    b. show interface-1
    c. show ip interface-1
    d. show access-list all

20. How do you verify a specific access list?
    a. show (number) access-list
    b. (number) show access-list
    c. show access list (number)
    d. show access-list (number)

21. Which of the following can be used to filter with an extended IP access list? (Select all that apply.)
    a. Port information
    b. Destination address
    c. Source address
    d. IP protocol
    e. All the above

22. You are setting up an IP extended access list using wildcard masking. "Any" is equivalent to saying 0.0.0.0 255.255.255.255. (T/F)
    a. True
    b. False

23. The extended IP access list uses the number range _____.
    a. 100-199
    b. 200-299
    c. 1-99
    d. 300-399

24. What will the line "deny telnet host 168.16.10.2 host 168.16.50.2 eq 23" do when working with an extended IP access list on interface s0 of 168.16.50.2?
    a. Allow all Telnet traffic from host 168.16.10.2 to enter interface s0
    b. Block all Telnet traffic from host 168.16.10.2 from entering interface s0
    c. Allow all Telnet traffic from host 168.16.50.2 to enter interface s0
    d. Block all Telnet traffic from host 168.16.50.2 from entering interface s0

Access Lists

25. The standard IPX access list uses which of the following number ranges?
    a. 1-99
    b. 100-199
    c. 1000-1099
    d. 800-899

26. Select one of the following options that represents a valid IPX standard access list.
    a. access-list 810 permit 40 30
    b. access-list 10 permit 40 30
    c. access-list 100 permit 40 30
    d. access-list 610 permit 40 30

27. Select four ways an extended Novell IPX access list can filter.
    a. Source network/node
    b. Destination network/node
    c. IPX protocol
    d. IPX socket
    e. IP source address

28. The extended IPX access list uses which of the following number ranges?
    a. 1-99
    b. 900-999
    c. 1000-1099
    d. 100-199

29. Which of the following is a correct access-list entry?
    a. Router(config-if)#access-list 1 permit 172.16.20.1 0.0.0.0
    b. Router(config)#access-list 1 permit 172.16.20.1 0.0.0.0
    c. Router#access-list 1 permit 172.16.20.1 0.0.0.0
    d. Router>access-list 1 permit 172.16.20.1 0.0.0.0

30. The SAP access list uses which number range?
    a. 1000-1099
    b. 1-99
    c. 900-999
    d. 300-399

31. The AppleTalk access list uses which number range?
    a. 600-699
    b. 900-999
    c. 1000-1099
    d. 300-399

Answers and Explanations

1. **d.** The commands used to view an IPX access list include: sh ipx e0, sh ipx ether0, and sh ipx int ether0. The commands are the same, but abbreviated differently.

2. **a.** There is an implied "deny all traffic" at the end of each access list. This means that if the packet does not meet the criteria in an access list, the packet will not be granted access and will be discarded.

3. **a.** If none of the entries in the access matches the packet, the implied "deny any" will be performed. Because of this, an access list must have one "permit" statement.

4. **a.** When creating an access list with a deny directive, it's important to add another line that allows all or some traffic, or you will just shut down the router.

5. **a.** As the packet enters the router, it is matched against the first statement in the access list. If a match is made in the first line entry of the access list, it performs the action (i.e., permit or deny). If a match is not made in the first statement of the access list, the packet will then be matched against the next entry, and so on. If none of the entries in the access matches the packet, the implied "deny any" will be performed. Because of this, an access list must have one "permit" statement.

6. **b.** If the packet does not match any of the conditions on the access list, the packet is discarded (the implied "deny" will be performed.)

7. **c.** If the packet does not match any of the conditions on the access list, the packet is discarded (the implied "deny" will be performed.)

8. **a.** Standard access lists can only filter based on the source address in the packet's IP header.

9. **d.** IP Standard Access List ranges from 1-99.

10. **a.** The access list is created in Global Configuration mode.

11. **c.** The key word is "deny", which will block all packets from the network 10.10.10.0.

12. **d.** The access-group command is defined at the interface level.

13. **a, b.** There are two steps in configuring a standard access list: Create the access list in Global Configuration mode, and apply the access list to the interface in Interface Configuration mode.

14. **a.** You can have only one access list per interface, per protocol, or per direction. This means you can have only one outbound or inbound access list per interface.

15. **a, c.** When configuring an access list to be applied to only one host, use 0.0.0.0 after the IP address or use the word "host". They would look like 172.12.30.55 0.0.0.0 or host 172.12.30.55. They both mean the same thing.

16. **c, d.** Two commands are used to view access lists: The show ip interface shows which interfaces have access lists set, and the show running-config command shows the access lists and which interfaces have access lists set.

17. **a.** The show ip interface command shows which interfaces have access lists set. If you view the IP access list on the serial 0 interface, you use the show ip interface s0 command.

18. **b.** The show access-list command will display all access lists configured on the router, access list numbers, and all the lines in them.

19. **a.** The show access-1 will list all the access lists configured on the router. If you want to view a specific access list, use the show access-list command followed by the access list number.

20. **d.** To view a specific access list, use the command show access-list (number).

21. **e.** Extended lists are used for packets entering or exiting an interface, and can filter based on the Source Address, Destination Address, IP protocol (TCP, UDP), and Port information.

22. **a.** The term "any" is the same as using the wildcards 0.0.0.0.255.255.255.255.

23. **a.** The number range for extended IP access lists is 100-199.

24. **b.** The key word is "deny", which will block traffic from host 168.16.10.2.

25. **d.** Standard IPX access list numbers must be between 800-899.

26. **a.** Access-list 810 is between 800-899 (Standard IPX access list).

27. **a, b, c, d.** Extended IPX access lists filter on the source network/node, destination network/node, IPX protocol (SAP, special), and IPX socket.

28. **b.** The extended IPX access list has a range of 900-999.

29. **b.** The level at which the access list is created is what's important. Answer B is correct, which creates the access list at the Global level.

30. **a.** The SAP access list has a range of 1000-1099.

31. **a.** The AppleTalk access list has a range of 600-699.

Chapter

Wide Area Networking

These are the areas that are generally testable on the CCNA examination:

Point-to-point leased lines:

- Differentiate between the following WAN services: Frame Relay, ISDN/LAPD, HDLC, and PPP.
- Configure authentication with PPP.
- Understand how Frame Relay works on a large WAN network.
- Configure Frame Relay LMIs, maps, and subinterfaces.
- Monitor Frame Relay operation in the router.
- Understand the ISDN protocols, function groups, and reference points.
- Describe how Cisco implements ISDN BRI.
- Identify PPP operations to encapsulate WAN data on Cisco routers.

Introduction

First, we'll define some basic Wide Area Networking (WAN) terms, which will help you better understand some of the features of WAN.

Next, you will learn the process and commands to enable PPP encapsulation on your router and the commands to enable CHAP and PAP on each interface.

You will also learn how to configure your router to use Frame Relay, and how mapping the IP address to the DLCI can be done dynamically with IARP or manually with the map command.

We'll look at the three LMI signaling standards. You will learn how to create a subinterface and then map IP addresses to the DLCIs.

Next we'll discuss the features of ISDN, which can carry voice, video, and data simultaneously, has a faster setup than a modem, and can transfer data faster than a modem. Finally, you'll learn about the characteristics of BRI and PRI.

BASIC WAN TERMS

- **Demarc:** Demarc is the boundary between the customer's in-house wiring and the service provider's wiring. Generally, a RJ-45 jack is located near the customer premise equipment. The CPE at this location would be a CSU/DSU or ISDN interface that plugs into the demarc.

- **CPE:** Customer premise equipment (CPE) is the wiring and equipment on the customer's side of the demarc.

- **Local loop:** The wiring running from the demarc to the CO.

- **CO (Central Office):** Usually called the POP (point of presence), this point is where the local loop gains access to the service provider's high-speed trunk lines.

- **Toll network:** Trunk lines inside a WAN provider's network. It is a collection of switches and facilities.

EXAM TIP: You need to know the definitions of these terms.

WAN Connection Types

- **Leased lines:** Also called point-to-point or dedicated connection. This is a pre-established WAN communication path from the CPE through the DCE switch, then to the CPE of the remote site. Leased lines allow DTE networks to communicate at any time with no setup procedures. It uses synchronous serial lines that can accommodate up to 45 Mbps.

- **Circuit switching:** Establishes communications similar to a phone call. Data cannot be transferred until the end-to-end connection is established. Circuit switching mainly uses dial-up modems and ISDN. It provides low-bandwidth data transfers.

- **Packet switching:** Provides shared bandwidth that allows a group of companies to reduce costs similar to old-style party-line telephones. Packet switching is a good choice for occasional bursty data transfers.

WAN Protocol Characteristics

- WAN protocols are used on point-to-point serial links and provide delivery service of data over those links.

- LAPB, HDLC, and PPP use framing to ensure that the receiving devices know where the beginning of the frame is, what address is in the header, and where the data portion begins. Framing must be used so the router receiving the data can determine which are the idle frames and how to process the data frames.

- Synchronous links are typically used between routers. Synchronous simply means that there is an imposed time ordering at the sending and receiving ends of the link, and the sides agree to a certain speed. Synchronous protocols allow more throughput over a serial link than do asynchronous. However, asynchronous protocols require less expensive hardware because there is no need to watch transitions and adjust the clock rate.

- Data-link protocols use error recovery to ensure data delivery. As data arrives, the Frame Check Sequence (FCS) field in the trailer is checked to verify if there were bit errors during transmission of the data. If an error is detected, the frame is discarded and the source will retransmit the frame.

WAN Terms Explained

- **ISDN (Integrated Services Digital Network):** *ISDN uses a digital service that transmits voice and data over telephone lines. *ISDN is used by remote users who have a need for a higher-speed connection than a normal analog dial-up link.*

- **HDLC (High-Level Data Link Control):** A low overhead connection-oriented, point-to-point protocol that operates at the Data Link layer and is used on leased lines. Authentication cannot be used. *HDLC is the default encapsulation used by Cisco routers over synchronous serial links.* It is proprietary to Cisco and can't communicate with any other vendor's HDLC implementation.

- **Frame Relay:** A high-performance specification that operates at the Data Link and Physical layers. Frame Relay is cheaper than point-to-point links and operates at speeds of 64 kbps to 1.544 Mbps. It also has dynamic-bandwidth allocation and congestion control. Frame Relay, however, does not provide error correction.

- **LAPB (Link Access Procedure, Balanced):** A Data Link layer connection-oriented protocol used with X.25. LAPB has a large overhead and should be used only if your link is troubled with a lot of errors.

- **PPP (Point-to-Point Protocol):** A widely accepted industry standard, PPP is used to create point-to-point links between different vendors' equipment. It allows authentication and multilink connections and can be run over asynchronous and synchronous links. PPP uses LCP (Link Control Protocol) to build and maintain data-link connections. It is used to transport layer-3 packets over a Data Link layer point-to-point link.

- **LCP:** Provides PPP encapsulation with these options:
    - **Authentication:** Two methods are PAP and CHAP
    - **Compression:** Used to increase throughput of the PPP connection.
    - **Error detection:** Used to ensure reliable transfer of data.
    - **Multilink:** Used to share the load over two or more parallel circuits.

It is important to note that the Network Control Protocol (NCP) is a component of PPP and is a method of establishing and configuring various Network-layer protocols.

NOTE: The same WAN data-link protocols must be on both sides of the serial link. If they are different, the router may not be able to process the information correctly.

- **Enabling PPP Encapsulation:** An example of how to enable PPP encapsulation on your router and enable CHAP or PAP on each interface:

    RouterA#**config t**
    RouterA(config)#**int s0**
    RouterA(config-if)#**encapsulation ppp**

    Router A#**config t**
    RouterA(config)#**int s0**
    RouterA(config-if)#**ppp authentication chap (or PAP)**

EXAM TIP: Know the process and commands to enable PPP encapsulation on your router and the commands to enable CHAP and PAP on each interface.

These are the areas that are generally testable on the CCNA examination:

Frame Relay protocols:

- Recognize key Frame Relay terms and features.

FRAME RELAY

Frame Relay provides a way for DTEs and DCEs to communicate. DTEs are usually terminals, PCs, routers, and bridges on the customer side. DCEs are usually carrier-owned devices. Frame Relay can use PVCs and SVCs, *but primarily uses PVCs only*. Frame Relay is a multi-access network that provides delivery of variable-sized data frames to multiple WAN-connected sites. Leased lines are used to connect Frame Relay networks. Frame Relay allows simultaneous transmission of voice, video, and data over a WAN connection.

Frame Relay terms and definitions:

- **VC (virtual circuit):** A logical path that a frame uses between DTEs.

- **PVC (permanent virtual circuit):** A VC that is a permanent connection.

- **SVC (switched virtual circuit):** A dynamically enabled VC. A SVC is similar to the way a dial connection is enabled.

- **DTE (data terminal equipment):** Sometimes called data-circuit termination equipment. Routers qualify as DTEs when they are connected to a Frame Relay service from a telecommunication company.

- **DCE (data communications equipment):** Frame Relay switches are DCE devices.

EXAM TIP: Know these terms and definitions. Also, know that Frame Relay usually uses only PVCs.

- **Data-Link Connection Identifier (DLCI) Addressing and Frame Relay Switching:** A DLCI is a Frame Relay address used to identify the DTEs that are to receive the frame. Your service provider will assign the DLCI to you. The DLCI is used to distinguish between different virtual circuits on the network.

The devices on each end of the virtual circuit must have their IP addresses mapped to the DLCIs. *Mapping the IP address to the DLCI can be done dynamically through IARP or manually through the Frame Relay map command.*

EXAM TIP: You need to know that mapping the IP address to the DLCI can be done dynamically with IARP or manually with the map command.

Enabling Frame Relay on the Router

When configuring Frame Relay on Cisco routers, you specify it as an encapsulation on serial interfaces. There are only two encapsulation types:

- Cisco
- IETF

```
RouterA(config)#int s0
RouterA(config)#encapsulation frame-relay ietf (or Cisco)
```

NOTE: *The default encapsulation is Cisco unless you type ietf. The Cisco encapsulation is used when two Cisco devices are connected together. When connecting your router to a non-Cisco device over Frame Relay, you will use IETF (Internet Engineering Task Force) encapsulation.*

Configuring DLCI Numbers

The command to establish DLCI numbers is as follows:

RouterA(config)#**int s0**
RouterA(config-if)#**frame-relay interface-dlci 16**

> EXAM TIP: Know how to enable Frame Relay on the router. Know the default encapsulation type: Use Cisco when connecting two Cisco devices together, IETF when connecting two non-Cisco routers. Then know how to configure DLCI numbers on an interface.

Local Management Interface

Local Management Interface (LMI) is a signaling standard used between a frame switch and a DTE device (router). LMI is a set of enhancements to the Frame Relay protocol. When configuring a Cisco router with an IOS prior to 11.2, you must specify the LMI type. IOS 11.2 and newer are set to autodetect the LMI type. Check with your Frame Relay ISP to find out the LMI type. There are three types of LMI:

- Cisco

- ANSI

- q933a

> EXAM TIP: Know these three LMI signaling standards.

The LMI provides a set of enhancements to the basic Frame Relay specification, including support for a keep-alive mechanism and statistics.

You can configure the following LMI-related parameters on the Frame Relay interface:

- LMI type
- LMI keep-alive interval
- LMI polling and timer intervals (optional)

Subinterfaces

Subinterfaces are created to allow you to have multiple virtual circuits on one serial interface. Different protocols can be assigned to each subinterface. These subinterfaces are considered separate interfaces.

Creating Subinterfaces

Subinterfaces are created with the **int s0.(subinterface number)** command. As shown below, you first set the encapsulation on the serial interface, then define the subinterface:

```
RouterA(config)#int s0
RouterA(config)#encapsulation frame-relay
RouterA(config)#int s0.18 point-to-point (or Multipoint)
```

Mapping DLCIs to IP Addresses in Frame Relay

IP addresses must be mapped to the DLCIs for both ends of a virtual circuit to communicate. *There are two ways to do this.*

```
RouterA(config)#int s0
RouterA(config-if)#encap frame
RouterA(config-if)#int s0.18 point-to-point
* RouterA(config-if)#no inverse-arp
RouterA(config-if)#ip address 192.40.20.1 255.255.255.0
RouterA(config-if)#frame-relay map ip 192.40.20.18 17
RouterA(config-if)#frame-relay map ip 192.40.20.19 18
```

EXAM TIP: Know how to create a subinterface and then map IP addresses to the DLCIs.

Inverse-ARP Function

If you do not want to manually map each virtual circuit, you can use the inverse-arp function to perform dynamic mapping of the IP address to the DLCI number. Here is how it is done:

RouterA(config)#**int s0.18 point-to-point**
RouterA(config-if)#**encap frame-relay ietf**
RouterA(config-if)#**ip address 192.40.20.1 255.255.255.0**

NOTE: Using the above does appear to be easier, but IARP is not as stable as the map command.

Committed Information Rate

On a Frame Relay network, each user is given a dedicated bandwidth that is guaranteed. When subscribing to Frame Relay, the ISP will guarantee you a minimum bandwidth that will always be available to you. This is called **Committed Information Rate (CIR)**. When the line is not saturated with traffic, you will be able to get a much higher transfer rate than the CIR. It gives the user the option to purchase a lower amount of bandwidth than what they normally might use.

EXAM TIP: Know what the CIR is.

Monitoring Frame Relay

- *Show frame-relay pvc:* Gives you a list of all configured PVCs and DLCI numbers (show running-config will also do this). It will also show you the status of each PVC connection and traffic statistics.

    RouterA#**show frame pvc**

- *Show int s0:* Shows the LMI traffic on interface s0.

    RouterA#**show int s0**

- ***Show frame-relay map:** Shows the IP address to DLCI mappings. This command is also used to monitor frame-relay activity of a Cisco router. sh int s0 can also be used to monitor frame-relay activity.

    RouterB#**show frame-relay map**

- **Show frame lmi:** Gives you the LMI traffic statistics between the local router and Frame Relay switch.

    Router#**sh frame lmi**

- **Clear frame-relay-inarp:** Clears dynamic mappings.

    RouterB#**clear frame-relay-inarp**

EXAM TIP: Know the highlighted (with an "*") commands above, for sure. Become familiar with the other commands.

These are the areas that are generally testable on the CCNA examination:

ISDN protocols and design:

- State a relevant use and content for ISDN networking.
- Identify ISDN protocols, function groups, reference points, and channels.

INTEGRATED SERVICES DIGITAL NETWORK

Integrated Services Digital Network (ISDN) is a digital service that runs on analog telephone networks. There are two types of ISDN interfaces:

- Basic Rate Interface (BRI)
- Primary Rate Interface (PRI)

Both BRI and PRI provide multiple digital bearer channels supporting data and voice.

PPP provides data encapsulation, link integrity, and authentication for the ISDN connection. *The characteristics of ISDN are as follows:*

- *BRI: has 2 (64 Kbps) B Channels and 1 (16 Kbps) D Channel.*
- *PRI: has 23 (64 Kbps) B Channels and 1 (64 Kbps) D Channel.*
- Carries voice, video, and data simultaneously.
- Has faster call setup than a modem.
- Has faster data rates than a modem connection.

> **EXAM TIP:** Know that ISDN can carry voice, video, and data simultaneously, has a faster setup than a modem, and can transfer data faster than a modem. An ISDN connection is the fastest and easiest to set up. Finally, know how many channels BRI and PRI have.

B channels are used to transport data and are therefore called bearer channels. D channels are used for signaling. As you configure ISDN BRI, you need to have one SPID (Service Profile Identifier) for each B channel.

To enable ISDN BRI you need to use the **isdn spid1 interface** subcommands. SPIDs are assigned to you by your ISDN provider. The SPIDs that are provided are actually used to identify your connection to the switch. The last part of the SPID subcommand is the local dial number for that SPID.

```
RouterA#config t
RouterA(config)#isdn switch-type basic-ne1
RouterA(config)#int bri0
RouterA(config-if)#encap ppp
RouterA(config-if)#isdn spid1 0754515521211 5678833
```

Dial-on-Demand Routing

Dial-on-Demand Routing (DDR) allows you to define interesting traffic on your router via access lists, and set up WAN links based on that traffic. DDR can lower costs derived from an ISP or telephone company by filtering only the traffic you wish to pass through the router. *The term "interesting traffic" is defined as the data that you want supported on your router*, compared to the "uninteresting traffic" that you don't want to support.

DDR requires static routes in order to function properly. When an interesting packet arrives at the router and a connection is not currently in use, the router will make a connection and the packet will be sent. However, if the packet is uninteresting, it will not match any entries in the access list and will be discarded. The last piece that can be configured for DDR is the Dialer Information.

ISDN protocols that you need to know include:

- **E-series** Uses ISDN on an existing telephone network.

- **I-series** Pertains to ISDN concepts, terminology, aspects, and services.

- **Q-series** Pertains to switching and signaling

EXAM TIP: Memorize these ISDN protocols and what they mean.

ISDN terminals:

- Devices connecting to an ISDN network are called terminal equipment (TE) and network termination (NT) equipment. The different types are:
    - TE1 – refers to the terminals that understand ISDN standards and can plug directly into the ISDN network.
    - TE2 – this type is older than ISDN standards. In order to use TE2 you have to have a terminal adapter (TA) to be able to plug into the ISDN network. This is sometimes called nonnative analog.
    - NT1 – this implements the ISDN Physical layer specifications and connects the user devices to the ISDN network.
    - NT2 – is typically a provider's equipment, like a switch.
    - TA – is a terminal adapter that converts TE2 wiring to TE1 wiring that then connects into an NT1 device.

EXAM TIP: Memorize these types of terminals and what they mean.

Wide Area Networking

The ISDN reference points used to define logical interfaces are as follows:

- **R reference point:** Defines the reference point between non-ISDN equipment and a terminal adapter (TA).

- **S reference point:** Defines the reference point between user terminals and an NT2.

- **T reference point:** Defines the reference point between NT1 and NT2 devices.

- **U reference point:** Defines the reference point between NT1 devices and line-termination equipment in a carrier network.

EXAM TIP: Learn the terms listed above.

Review Questions

1. Most Frame Relay networks use which of the following?
   a. PVCs
   b. SVCs
   c. VCs
   d. PPVCs

2. When connecting a Cisco router to another Cisco device using Frame Relay, which encapsulation type do you use?
   a. IETF
   b. Cisco
   c. Ansi
   d. Q933a

3. When connecting a Cisco router to a non-Cisco device using Frame Relay, which encapsulation type do you use?
   a. IETF
   b. Cisco
   c. Ansi
   d. Q933a

4. Which of these are types of Local Management Interface (LMI)? (Select all that apply.)
    a. Cisco
    b. ANSI
    c. q933a (May be listed as ITU-T or CCITT)
    d. All the above

5. Which statements describe default encapsulation configuration? (Select two.)
    a. IETF encapsulation must be configured unless the connecting routers are both Cisco.
    b. Cisco encapsulation must be configured unless the connecting routers are both IETF.
    c. The default encapsulation is Cisco.
    d. IETF is the default encapsulation.

6. Which statements are correct concerning ISDN? (Select two.)
    a. ISDN can accommodate voice only.
    b. ISDN BRI carries 23 B channels and 1 D channel.
    c. ISDN can accommodate both voice and data communications.
    d. ISDN PRI carries 23 B channels and 1 D channel.

7. Protocols that end with the letter _____ specify ISDN on an existing telephone network.
    a. E
    b. I
    c. Q
    d. U

8. Protocols that end with the letter _____ specify concepts, terminology, and services.
    a. E
    b. I
    c. Q
    d. U

9. Protocols that end with the letter _____ specify switching and signaling.
   a. E
   b. I
   c. Q
   d. U

10. Which ISDN reference point describes the point between non-ISDN equipment and a TA?
    a. The R reference point
    b. The T reference point
    c. The S reference point
    d. The U reference point

11. Which ISDN reference point describes the point between NT1 and NT2 devices?
    a. The R reference point
    b. The T reference point
    c. The S reference point
    d. The U reference point

12. Which ISDN reference point describes the point between user terminals and NT2?
    a. The R reference point
    b. The T reference point
    c. The S reference point
    d. The U reference point

13. Which ISDN reference point describes the point between NT1 devices and line-termination equipment in a carrier network?
    a. The R reference point
    b. The T reference point
    c. The S reference point
    d. The U reference point

14. Which of the following statements is true?
    a. CIR has a guaranteed minimum bandwidth.
    b. CIR has a guaranteed maximum bandwidth.
    c. CIR stands for the communication internetworking rate.
    d. None of the above

15. Which command can show you the DLCIs?
    a. show dlci
    b. show hosts
    c. show ip int
    d. show frame-relay map

16. Which of the following are steps to configure DDR?
    a. Define static routes
    b. Specify interesting traffic
    c. Configure the dialer information
    d. All the above

17. Which commands are used to monitor Frame Relay activity on a Cisco router? (Select two.)
    a. show ip route
    b. show frame-relay activity
    c. show interface s0
    d. show frame-relay map

Answers and Explanations

1. **a.** Frame Relay can use PVCs and SVCs, but primarily uses PVCs only.

2. **b.** The Cisco encapsulation is used when two Cisco devices are connected together.

3. **a.** When connecting a Cisco router to a non-Cisco device over Frame Relay, the IETF (Internet Engineering Task Force) encapsulation is used.

4. **d.** Local Management Interface is a set of enhancements to the Frame Relay protocol. There are three types of LMI. They are Cisco, ANSI, and q933a. When configuring a Cisco router with an IOS prior to 11.2, you must specify the LMI type. IOS 11.2 and newer are set to autodetect the LMI type.

5. **a, c.** The default encapsulation is Cisco unless you type ietf. The Cisco encapsulation is used when two Cisco devices are connected together. When connecting your router to a non-Cisco device over Frame Relay, you will use IETF (Internet Engineering Task Force) encapsulation.

6. **c, d.** ISDN uses a digital service that transmits voice and data over telephone lines. The Primary Rate Interface (PRI) of ISDN has 23 (64 kbps) B Channels and 1 (64 kbps) D Channel. B channels are used to transport data and are therefore called bearer channels. D channels are used for signaling.

7. **a.** E-series ISDN protocols specify ISDN on an existing telephone network.

8. **b.** I-series ISDN protocols specify ISDN concepts, aspects, and interfaces.

9 **c.** Q-series ISDN protocols specify switching and signaling.

10. **a.** The R reference point defines the reference point between non-ISDN equipment and a terminal adapter (TA).

11. **b.** The T reference point defines the reference point between NT1 and NT2 devices.

12. **c.** The S reference point defines the reference point between user terminals and an NT2.

13. **d.** The U reference point defines the reference point between NT1 devices and line-termination equipment in a carrier network.

14. **a.** When subscribing to Frame Relay, the ISP will guarantee you a minimum bandwidth that will always be available to you. This is called Committed Information Rate (CIR).

15. **d.** The show frame-relay map command shows the IP address to DLCI mappings.

16. **d.** DDR requires static routes in order to function properly. When an interesting packet arrives at the router and a connection is not currently in use, the router will make a connection and the packet will be sent. However, if the packet is uninteresting, it will not match any entries in the access list and will be discarded. The last piece that can be configured for DDR is the Dialer Information.

17. **c, d.** Show interface shows the status of the interface and line protocol. Show frame-relay map shows the IP address to DLCI mappings.

Index

CCNA Exam Preparation

Index

TIFF, 7
Time to live (TTL), 120
Toll network, 203
Traceroute, 120
Translation services, 7
Transport, 19
Transport layer, 9, 11
Triggered updates, 154
Trunk links, 58
Trunks, 59

U

U reference point, 214
UDP, 9, 114
Undebug ip rip, 156
Unique IP address, 121
Unreliable, 118
Unreliable connection, 6
Unsequenced, 118
Upper layers, 5
User Datagram Protocol (UDP), 117
User mode, 68, 70
UTP (Unshielded Twisted Pair), 24

V

V.24, 18
V.35, 18
VC (virtual circuit), 206
Virtual circuit, 118
Virtual circuit management, 9
Virtual LAN, 16, 55
Virtual terminal password, 75
VLAN Trunk Protocol (VTP), 59
VLANs, 56-57
VTP modes, 59

W

WAN protocols, 17
Wildcard masking, 183
Wire speed, 39

X

X Windows, 7
X.21, 18